William Damon, *Brown University*
EDITOR-IN-CHIEF

Romantic Relationships in Adolescence: Developmental Perspectives

Shmuel Shulman
Bar Ilan University, Ramat Gan, Israel
W. Andrew Collins
University of Minnesota

EDITORS

Number 78, Winter 1997

JOSSEY-BASS PUBLISHERS
San Francisco

ROMANTIC RELATIONSHIPS IN ADOLESCENCE: DEVELOPMENTAL PERSPECTIVES
Shmuel Shulman, W. Andrew Collins (eds.)
New Directions for Child Development, no. 78
William Damon, Editor-in-Chief

Microfilm copies of issues and articles are available in 16mm and 35mm, as well as microfiche in 105mm, through University Microfilms Inc., 300 North Zeeb Road, Ann Arbor, Michigan 48106–1346.

ISSN 0195-2269   ISBN 0-7879-4124-7

NEW DIRECTIONS FOR CHILD DEVELOPMENT is part of The Jossey-Bass Education Series and is published quarterly by Jossey-Bass Inc., Publishers, 350 Sansome Street, San Francisco, California 94104–1342. Periodicals postage paid at San Francisco, California, and at additional mailing offices. Postmaster: Send address changes to New Directions for Child Development, Jossey-Bass Inc., Publishers, 350 Sansome Street, San Francisco, California 94104-1342.

New Directions for Child Development® is indexed in Biosciences Information Service, Current Index to Journals in Education (ERIC), Psychological Abstracts, and Sociological Abstracts.

SUBSCRIPTIONS cost $65.00 for individuals and $105.00 for institutions, agencies, and libraries.

EDITORIAL CORRESPONDENCE should be sent to the Editor-in-Chief, William Damon, Department of Education, Box 1938, Brown University, Providence, Rhode Island 02912.

Cover photograph by Wernher Krutein/PHOTOVAULT © 1990.

Jossey-Bass Web address: http://www.josseybass.com

Manufactured in the United States using Lyons Falls D'Anthology paper, which is a special blend of non-tree fibers and totally chlorine-free wood pulp.

CONTENTS

EDITORS' NOTES

Although there is a sizeable literature on romantic relationships in the college years and adulthood, limited research exists on romantic relationships in adolescence. The extant work consists primarily of demographic studies of dating patterns and deals little with aspects such as the characteristics or development of adolescent romantic relationships. Particularly lacking is a theoretical framework to guide research on romantic relationships during this developmental stage. It is especially difficult to understand this lacuna because early romantic relationships are believed to play a role in the consolidation of identity and may affect subsequent romantic relationships and marital life.

The present volume, *Romantic Relationships in Adolescence,* offers both innovative research and compelling discussion that advance understanding of the development and course of romantic relationships in adolescence. Brett Laursen and Vickie A. Williams, in Chapter One, present a descriptive account of the developmental variations in adolescent close relationships with family members, friends, and romantic partners. Within the context of social exchange theory, they show how closeness shifts from parents to peers and romantic partners. In Chapter Two, Wyndol Furman and Elizabeth A. Wehner present a theoretical framework that extends our understanding of the developmental changes in romantic relationships by comparing the functioning of romantic partners and significant others in the attachment, caregiving, and affiliative systems. The authors indicate the need for assessing these changes in light of unconscious perceptions. In Chapter Three, Shmuel Shulman, Rachel Levy-Shiff, Peri Kedem, and Eitan Alon examine adolescent romantic relationships in terms of intimacy emerging from a systems theory. Their findings point to qualitative differences in adolescent romantic relationships and show that the development of an intimate romantic relationship requires a greater commitment in males than in females.

In Chapter Four, Inge Seiffge-Krenke's longitudinal data follow the balancing of intimacy and conflict in romantic relationships among healthy and diabetic adolescents. Her findings shed light on the difficulties that diabetic adolescents have in facing both positive and negative experiences in their romantic relationships. In Chapter Five, W. Andrew Collins, Katherine C. Hennighausen, David Taylor Schmit, and L. Alan Sroufe present one of the first studies to examine the precursors of romantic relationships with a special emphasis on the quality of early mother-child and peer relationships. Campbell Leaper and Kristin J. Anderson present a comprehensive conceptual review of cross-gender friendships in Chapter Six. They also discuss what can be learned from these friendships to improve romantic relationships. In Chapter Seven, Shmuel Shulman, W. Andrew Collins, and Danielle Knafo discuss essential issues in the understanding and study of processes and development of adolescent romantic relationships.

This volume grew out of the symposium "International Perspectives on Romantic Relationships in Adolescence: Characterizations and Conceptualizations" presented at the 1996 biennial meeting of the Society for Research on Adolescence, held in Boston. W. Andrew Collins, Katherine C. Hennighausen, David Taylor Schmit, and L. Alan Sroufe graciously agreed to join the participants from that symposium by contributing to the volume. Wyndol Furman, a participant in the symposium, and Elizabeth A. Wehner were kind enough to write a special chapter for this issue.

We express our appreciation to each of the authors as well as to series editor-in-chief William Damon. All were unfailingly cooperative, some despite personal adversity and time pressures.

Shmuel Shulman
W. Andrew Collins
Editors

SHMUEL SHULMAN is associate professor in the Department of Psychology at Bar Ilan University, Ramat Gan, Israel.

W. ANDREW COLLINS is professor at the Institute of Child Development, University of Minnesota.

Adolescents' relationships with mothers, fathers, siblings, friends, and romantic partners are examined. Across the adolescent years, interdependence (operationalized in terms of social interaction, activities, and influence) and perceived closeness shift from parents to peers, with patterns that differ somewhat for adolescents with and without a romantic partner. The findings are discussed in the context of social exchange theory, which offers a descriptive account of developmental variations in adolescent close relationships.

Perceptions of Interdependence and Closeness in Family and Peer Relationships Among Adolescents With and Without Romantic Partners

Brett Laursen, Vickie A. Williams

Social exchange theory (Kelley and Thibaut, 1978) offers a compelling description of interpersonal relationships, their development, and their maintenance. By this account, close relationships are organized on the basis of interdependence in the thoughts, emotions, and behaviors of participants (Kelley and others, 1983). Considerable research supports the notion that interdependence plays a key role in adult romantic and marital relationships (see Clark and Reis, 1988, for review). Less is known, however, about interdependence within other relationships and during other age periods. This investigation describes changes in important markers of interdependence across the adolescent years, extending social exchange theory to developmental variations in family and peer relationships. Of particular interest are age-related alterations in relationships and the extent to which participation in a romantic relationship is associated with different patterns of interdependence with family members and friends.

Support for this research was provided by a Johann Jacobs Foundation Young Investigator Award to Brett Laursen. Support for the preparation of this chapter was provided by a grant to Brett Laursen from the U.S. National Institute of Child Health and Human Development (R29-HD33006). Special thanks to David G. Perry for his thoughtful comments and to Michael Hayes, Mary Jane McAninch, Elizabeth Norton, and Sandra Sagba for assistance with data collection and coding. Correspondence should be directed to Brett Laursen, Florida Atlantic University, 2912 College Avenue, Fort Lauderdale, Florida, 33314–7714, USA. Electronic mail should be addressed to LAURSEN@ACC.FAU.EDU.

Interdependence is conceptually similar to *closeness:* the former emphasizes the processes and properties of social exchanges, whereas the latter focuses on their content and quality. An emphasis on process distinguishes interdependence frameworks from frameworks oriented toward the type of resources provided by a relationship (Foa, 1973) and the affective correlates afforded by affiliation (Rubin, 1973). Social exchange theory is predicated on the notion that individuals seek to maximize positive outcomes in relationships (Kelley and Thibaut, 1978). Mutually beneficial exchanges promote interdependence as participants come to rely on one another for rewards. In close relationships, interdependence is evident in frequent, strong, and diverse interconnections between participants (Kelley and others, 1983). These interconnections, which provide an objective index of interdependence, feature prominently in contemporary measures of the construct. Consistent with this research tradition, the work described in this chapter assays interdependence in terms of participant interconnections.

Relationships differ in the degree to which interdependence is salient. *Communal* and *exchange* relationships entail different types of interdependence (Clark and Mills, 1979). Communal relationships, with romantic partners, family members, and friends, assume mutual need fulfillment, regardless of imbalance in the costs and benefits accruing to participants. Exchange relationships, with classmates, neighbors, and business associates, assume equitable costs and benefits, regardless of imbalance in participant needs. *Voluntary* and *involuntary* relationships differ in terms of the significance of interdependence (Berscheid, 1985). In voluntary associations, with friends and romantic partners, interdependence is a primary concern because participants are free to dissolve inequitable relationships. In involuntary associations, with family members, customs and law often take precedence over interdependence considerations. *Horizontal* and *vertical* relationships, which differ in terms of reciprocity and the distribution of power, entail distinct processes of social exchange (Hartup and Laursen, 1991). In horizontal relationships, with friends, romantic partners, and classmates, participants must agree on exchange outcomes, which tends to encourage equity. In vertical relationships, with parents, teachers, and employers, one participant may unilaterally determine exchange outcomes, which suggests that equity is not an overriding concern.

Manifestations of interdependence vary across relationships. College students and adults report greater interdependence in communal than in exchange relationships (Argyle and Furnham, 1983; Berscheid, Snyder, and Omoto, 1989b). Children evaluate social exchange requirements in voluntary and horizontal relationships differently than in involuntary and vertical relationships, behaving in a manner consistent with these evaluations (Graziano, Musser, Rosen, and Shaffer, 1984). This evidence suggests that voluntary, horizontal, and communal relationships are guided by principles of social exchange, whereas other types of relationships appear to be organized according to different priorities.

Developmental alterations are anticipated as adolescent interdependence shifts from the family to peers. These changes may be the result of maturation and experience, contributing to a more sophisticated appreciation of social exchange principles (Graziano, 1984). Expectations formed by children about interdependent relationships are typically reconsidered during adolescence (Collins and Repinski, 1994). The emergence of close friendships and romantic relationships coincides with adolescent identity development and the normative push for autonomy from parents; these factors create strong social pressures to revise patterns of social interaction (Brown, in press). Alterations are also anticipated in adolescent social exchanges as environmental constraints on peer relationships decline; less adult supervision produces greater interdependence among friends and romantic partners as interconnections expand (Laursen, 1996). Increasing experience in and awareness of peer relationships should change parent-child relationships as preferences for reciprocal social exchanges create pressures for vertical relationships to realign in a manner that resembles horizontal relationships (Youniss, 1980).

As noted earlier, interdependence presumes frequent, diverse, and influential exchanges (Kelley and others, 1983). Although developmental research has yet to examine interdependence directly, several studies of its constituent components indicate change in adolescent relationships. Companionship and the amount of time spent with parents, siblings, and same-sex friends decreases across adolescence, whereas that with opposite-sex friends increases (Clark-Lempers, Lempers, and Ho, 1991; Larson and Richards, 1991). Control and unilateral influence by parents and same-sex friends peak in early to mid-adolescence; shared and mutual influence in these relationships increase across adolescence (Hunter and Youniss, 1982). Perceived power relative to parents declines across adolescence, power relative to siblings and same-sex friends increases across adolescence, and power relative to romantic partners remains unchanged (Furman and Buhrmester, 1992).

Building on these developmental depictions, the present investigation aims to expand depictions of interconnections in adolescent relationships and to determine the extent to which participation in romantic relationships is associated with different patterns of interdependence in relationships with family members and friends. Using an instrument specifically designed to assess interdependence—the Relationship Closeness Inventory (RCI) (Berscheid and others, 1989b)—interconnections between participants in a relationship are described along three dimensions: interaction frequency, activity diversity, and influence strength. Interdependence is operationally defined as the sum of standardized scores for each variable. As a paper-and-pencil measure of unilateral perceptions of the relationship, the instrument provides a rough approximation of interdependence. Even so, the interconnections assayed are conceptually consistent with the core behavioral constructs of interdependence as identified by Kelley and his colleagues (1983), and as a consequence the RCI is considered one of the best measures of interdependence available. The questionnaire differs from others applied to adolescent relationships in that affect is not conflated with interconnected behaviors, and the frequency, diversity, and influence of social exchanges are assessed concurrently. The RCI affords a unique perspective on close relationships, one that has hitherto been applied only to adult relationships: interdependence captures important distinctions among relationships, yet is distinct from emotional tone, liking, loving, and closeness (Berscheid, Snyder, and Omoto, 1989a).

Adolescents eleven to nineteen years old described closeness and aspects of interdependence with mothers, fathers, siblings, friends, and romantic partners. Three questions are addressed in this study:

1. *Do relationship interdependence and closeness differ across adolescence?* Although this is one of the first investigations of adolescent interdependence (as operationalized in the RCI), data from other sources (Furman and Buhrmester, 1992; Larson and Richards, 1991) suggest that indices of companionship (such as social interaction and activity diversity) and closeness with family members should decline, while that with friends and romantic partners should increase.

2. *Do adolescents with romantic partners report less interdependence and closeness with family and friends than adolescents without romantic partners?* Little is known about how romantic relationships alter other adolescent relationships, although some researchers have suggested that closeness and companionship with family members and friends must inevitably decline as the salience of romantic relationships increases (Brown, in press).

3. *Do adolescents perceive relationships with the greatest levels of interdependence to be their closest relationships?* Research suggests that objectively defined reports of adult interdependence differ somewhat from the more subjective experience of closeness (Berscheid, Snyder, and Omoto, 1989a); a similar set of distinct but overlapping impressions of relationship interdependence and closeness are expected during adolescence.

Method

A measure of interdependence originally developed for college students was administered to a sample of adolescents ranging from eleven to nineteen years old. One of the first studies to assess interdependence and closeness in adolescent relationships, this study provides support for the validity of a modified RCI that may be used with younger populations.

Participants. The participants were 245 (102 males and 143 females) Anglo Americans from rural New England public schools. The total included 105 (45 males and 60 females) seventh graders, ages 12 to 14 (M = 12.5 years old); 36 (11 males and 25 females) ninth graders, ages 14 to 16 (M = 14.5 years old); 29 (11 males and 18 females) tenth and eleventh graders, ages 15 to 17 (M = 16.2 years old); and 75 (35 males and 40 females) twelfth graders, ages 17 to 19 (M = 17.5 years old). All students attending homerooms and study halls (twelfth graders were overrepresented in the latter, seventh graders in the former) were invited to participate. Rates of participation ranged from 48 percent to 67 percent.

A total of 299 adolescents returned questionnaires, but 54 were eliminated because data were missing or subjects did not participate in one of the target relationships. Thus the final subject pool included 245 adolescents completing questionnaires describing two parents, a sibling, and a friend. Of these participants, 233 lived with a mother (or stepmother), 198 lived with a father (or stepfather), and 173 lived with a sibling (or stepsibling). This sample of 245 included reports describing three stepmothers, twenty-nine stepfathers, and eighteen stepsiblings.

Of the 245 participants in the investigation, 118 reported a romantic relationship. The proportion of adolescents with a romantic partner was similar for males (45.1 percent, $n = 46$) and females (50.3 percent, $n = 72$). Rates of participation in a romantic relationship increased from 34.3 percent ($n = 36$) in seventh grade and 30.6 percent ($n = 11$) in ninth grade to 58.6 percent ($n = 17$) in tenth and eleventh grade and 72.0 percent ($n = 54$) in twelfth grade.

Procedure. During a single class period, groups of adolescents completed five counterbalanced versions of a modified RCI (Berscheid, Snyder, and Omoto, 1989b), one each for mothers (or stepmothers), fathers (or stepfathers), closest age siblings (or stepsiblings), same-sex best friends, and romantic partners. Adolescents were instructed to skip questionnaires concerning relationships in which they did not participate. Each RCI contained three subscales:

1. *Interaction frequency:* the number of minutes participants in a relationship spent alone together in social interaction during the morning, afternoon, and evening of a typical day (range: 0 to 1,200 minutes)

2. *Activity diversity:* the number of different activities (from a thirty-eight-item checklist) that participants in a relationship engaged in alone together during the previous week (range: 0 to 38 activities). Six original items were modified for use with adolescent subjects: engaged in sexual relations, went to an auction or antique show, went to a bar, went on an outing, cleaned house or apartment, and planned a party or social event were respectively changed to displayed affection, went to the mall, went to a bar or alcohol-free club, went to the park or beach, did chores, and spent time on hobbies.

3. *Influence strength:* ratings (from a thirty-four-item inventory) of the partner's perceived influence over the adolescent's thoughts, feelings, and behaviors (range: 34 to 238). Items were scored on a seven-point scale ranging from strongly disagree (1) to strongly agree (7). Four original items were modified for use with adolescent subjects: time I devote to my career, the type of career I have, my future financial security, and my present financial security were respectively changed to time I devote to my studies, my selection of courses or major, the amount of money I will have in the future, and the amount of money I have now.

Intercorrelations indicated that the three subscales were only modestly associated. Pearson's correlation r (all p's < .05), calculated across grades, examined associations among interaction frequency, activity diversity, and influence strength within each adolescent relationship. For mothers, activity diversity was linked to interaction frequency ($r = .21$) and influence strength ($r = .27$). For fathers, interaction frequency was associated with activity diversity

($r = .48$) and influence strength ($r = .19$), and activity diversity was linked to influence strength ($r = .32$). For siblings, activity diversity was correlated with interaction frequency ($r = .41$) and influence strength ($r = .27$). For friends, activity diversity was associated with interaction frequency ($r = .40$) and influence strength ($r = .28$). For romantic partners, interaction frequency was associated with activity diversity ($r = .35$) and influence strength ($r = .32$), and activity diversity was linked to influence strength ($r = .38$). In sum, the number of different weekly activities was associated with the amount of daily social interaction and the level of perceived influence in each adolescent relationships, but influence and social interaction were linked only in relationships with fathers and romantic partners.

Interdependence was defined as the sum of converted scores for interaction frequency, activity diversity, and influence strength. Raw scores on these subscales were converted to a standard ten-point scale and summed (range: 3 to 30). For each subject, the relationship with the greatest total score was designated interdependent (Berscheid, Snyder, and Omoto, 1989b). All of the relationships included in this survey contained some degree of interdependence, so this label is shorthand for the relationship with the most interdependence as measured by the RCI.

Closeness describes responses to a checklist (Berscheid, Snyder, and Omoto, 1989a) containing twelve relationships (mother, father, sibling, best friend, romantic partner, teacher, aunt or uncle, cousin, grandparent, coach or extracurricular activity sponsor, employer, and coworker). For each subject, the relationship selected as the closest (identify the person with whom you have the closest, deepest, most involved and most intimate relationship) was designated close. All of the relationships included in this survey contained some degree of closeness, so this label is shorthand for subject reports of the perceived closest relationship.

Concordance describes the match between individual reports of close and interdependent relationships. Agreement indicates that both measures identified the same relationship, disagreement indicates that different close and interdependent relationships emerged.

Adequate RCI test-retest reliability (rs = .61 to .82) and internal subscale reliability (alphas = .56 to .87) have been reported in samples of college students (Berscheid, Snyder, and Omoto, 1989b). Previous findings suggest significant associations between partners' perceptions of romantic relationships (rs = .34 to .43) during young adulthood and between partners' perceptions of same-sex (but not opposite-sex) parent-child relationships (rs = .35 to .52) during adolescence (Berscheid, Snyder, and Omoto, 1989b; Repinski, 1993). In a pilot study with the modified RCI from the present investigation, internal subscale reliability (alphas = .79 to .91) was evident for each relationship in seventh grade through college undergraduate samples (Wilder, 1995).

Plan of Analyses. The first analyses describe characteristics of interdependence. Comparisons examine whether aspects of interdependence differ across adolescence and between relationships, and whether these patterns vary for adolescents with and without romantic partners. MANOVAs (multiple analyses of variance) and ANOVAs (analyses of variance) determine grade, sex, and romantic partner status differences in the interaction frequency, activity diversity, and influence strength of adolescent relationships. Degrees of freedom are adjusted conservatively (from approximately 1,200 to 200) in repeated measures analyses, substituting the number of subjects (minus the number of conditions) for the larger number of subjects multiplied by the number of conditions. Degrees of freedom differ slightly because of variations in missing data. Follow-up paired t-tests (within subjects) and Tukey's contrasts (between subjects) elaborate relationship and group differences, respectively.

The second analyses concern close and interdependent relationships. These comparisons examine whether relationships identified as close and interdependent differ from one another, differ across grades, and differ as a function of participation in romantic relationships. Chi-square contrasts determine grade, sex, and romantic partner status differences in close relationships, interdependent relationships, and measurement concordance.

The analyses were repeated three times to replicate the results reported in the text. The first repetition involved 299 adolescents, including 54 participants without a mother (or stepmother), father (or stepfather), sibling (or stepsibling), or friend. The second involved 142 adolescents residing with both parents and a sibling, excluding 103 participants not living with a mother (or stepmother), father (or stepfather), and sibling (or stepsibling). The third involved 201 adolescents reporting biological parents and siblings, excluding 44 participants with stepmothers, stepfathers, or stepsiblings. Findings from these samples and the 245 adolescents with two parents, a sibling, and a friend were virtually identical.

Results

The first analyses quantify characteristics of interdependence in adolescent relationships, with contrasts elaborating interaction frequency, activity diversity, and influence strength with mothers, fathers, siblings, friends, and romantic partners. The second analyses concern qualitative features of adolescent relationships, with contrasts exploring distinctions between relationships selected as close and relationships emerging as interdependent from RCI assessments of interconnections between participants.

Interdependence Characteristics. A repeated measures MANOVA was conducted with three between-subject independent variables of grade (seventh, ninth, tenth and eleventh, and twelfth), sex (male and female), and romantic partner status (present and absent), and one within-subject independent variable of relationships (mother, father, sibling, and friend). The three interdependence characteristics (interaction frequency, activity diversity, and influence strength) were the dependent variables. Main effects emerged for grade, $F(3, 197) = 7.25$, $p < .001$; and for relationships, $F(3, 164) = 11.21$, $p < .001$. There were also two-way interactions between interdependence characteristics and grade, $F(6, 180) = 3.27$, $p < .01$; between interdependence characteristics and sex, $F(2, 180) = 7.21$, $p < .001$; and between interdependence characteristics and relationships, $F(6, 116) = 16.94$, $p < .001$. And there were three-way interactions for grade, sex, and romantic partner status, $F(3, 197) = 2.96$, $p < .05$; for relationships, sex, and romantic partner status, $F(3, 164) = 4.08$, $p < .01$; and for interdependence characteristics, sex, and romantic partner status, $F(2, 180) = 4.87$, $p < .01$.

Separate analyses considered interaction frequency, activity diversity, and influence strength. In each case, follow-up comparisons of relationship differences involved 245 participants in contrasts among mothers, fathers, siblings, and friends, and 118 participants in contrasts of romantic partners with mothers, fathers, siblings, and friends.

Interaction Frequency. An ANOVA was conducted with three between-subject independent variables of grade, sex, and romantic partner status, and one within-subject independent variable of relationships. Interaction frequency was the dependent variable. Main effects emerged for grade, $F(3, 221) = 5.16$, $p < .01$; and for relationships, $F(3, 188) = 6.07$, $p < .001$. There was also a three-way interaction for relationships, sex, and romantic partner status, $F(3, 188) = 3.45$, $p < .05$. Tukey's contrasts (p's $< .05$) indicated that twelfth graders (M = 71.8, SD = 47.6) reported less average social interaction than seventh graders (M = 96.6, SD = 67.9), with ninth graders (M = 84.1, SD = 67.5) and tenth and eleventh graders (M = 76.5, SD = 57.1) in between.

Two separate ANOVAs explored the three-way interaction of relationships, sex, and romantic partner status. The first included adolescents with romantic partners ($n = 118$) and the second involved adolescents without romantic partners ($n = 127$). Each ANOVA entailed two between-subject independent variables of grade and sex, and one within-subject independent variable of relationships. Interaction frequency was the dependent variable.

In analyses of adolescents with romantic partners, main effects emerged for sex, $F(1, 106) = 11.57$, $p < .001$; and for relationships, $F(4, 81) = 9.23$, $p < .001$. There were also two-way interactions between relationships and grade, $F(12, 81) = 5.91$, $p < .001$; and between relationships and sex, $F(4, 81) = 4.69$, $p < .001$. Follow-up ANOVAs, conducted separately for each grade, revealed relationship main effects (p's $< .001$) for seventh graders, tenth and eleventh graders, and twelfth graders. Paired t-tests indicated that social interaction among seventh graders was greatest with siblings and mothers, whereas tenth, eleventh, and twelfth graders reported social interaction to be most frequent with romantic partners. Follow-up ANOVAs, conducted separately for each sex, revealed relationship main effects (p's $< .01$) for males and females. Paired t-tests indicated that males reported social interaction to be most frequent with romantic partners, whereas females reported the greatest levels of social interaction with mothers, romantic partners, and friends (see Table 1.1). In analyses of adolescents without romantic partners, there were neither statistically significant main effects nor interactions involving the frequency of daily social interaction (see Table 1.1).

Table 1.1. Daily Interaction Frequency (in Minutes) Within Adolescent Relationships

	Relationship				
	Mother M (SD)	Father M (SD)	Sibling M (SD)	Friend M (SD)	Romantic Partner M (SD)
	Adolescents with Romantic Partners				
Grade					
7th	119.7[a]	76.6[b]	124.9[a]	99.1[ab]	41.4[c]
	(100.2)	(86.2)	(124.6)	(100.2)	(36.4)
9th	94.7	43.3	63.5	94.6	115.8
	(134.6)	(41.7)	(110.5)	(96.6)	(175.7)
10th/11th	73.5[b]	25.1[c]	61.2[bc]	72.6[b]	162.9[a]
	(80.6)	(27.3)	(102.3)	(78.2)	(185.8)
12th	76.1[b]	32.8[d]	52.6[c]	67.0[bc]	125.3[a]
	(73.6)	(35.1)	(61.9)	(84.4)	(127.9)
Sex					
Male	86.3[ab]	54.1[c]	107.3[ab]	75.0[bc]	133.8[a]
	(96.4)	(62.1)	(123.3)	(105.4)	(163.5)
Female	93.1[a]	40.1[c]	56.6[b]	82.9[a]	85.4[ab]
	(88.0)	(55.2)	(74.1)	(78.8)	(101.5)
Total	90.5	45.5	76.5	79.8	104.6
	(91.0)	(58.1)	(99.1)	(89.7)	(131.2)
	Adolescents Without Romantic Partners				
Grade					
7th	135.4	78.8	101.3	79.3	
	(140.7)	(97.6)	(98.3)	(101.7)	
9th	97.9	68.9	75.2	116.8	
	(93.3)	(100.6)	(75.8)	(137.8)	
10th/11th	74.5	65.6	72.0	79.7	
	(63.1)	(61.8)	(86.4)	(75.5)	
12th	71.0	55.9	92.5	78.0	
	(48.1)	(62.8)	(112.3)	(70.2)	
Sex					
Male	106.8	90.0	88.7	81.4	
	(133.1)	(107.6)	(94.5)	(99.7)	
Female	114.7	57.7	94.3	90.7	
	(103.6)	(71.0)	(96.7)	(106.9)	
Total	111.2	71.8	91.9	86.6	
	(117.1)	(89.9)	(95.4)	(103.5)	

Note: Separate analyses were conducted for adolescents with romantic partners ($n = 118$) and adolescents without romantic partners ($n = 127$). Within each grade and sex (rows), different superscripts denote significant ($P < .05$) relationship differences in paired t-tests.

To summarize, among those in romantic relationships, older adolescents and males interacted most frequently with romantic partners, whereas younger adolescents and females divided social interaction among several relationships; among adolescents without romantic relationships, there were no differences in rates of social interaction with mothers, fathers, siblings, and friends. Within each grade, adolescents without romantic partners reported greater daily social interaction in most family and friend relationships than adolescents with romantic partners. When scores are collapsed across grades, adolescents without romantic partners reported an average of almost 68 minutes more daily social interaction with family members and friends than adolescents with romantic partners, which works out to an additional 6.3 minutes with friends, 15.0 minutes with siblings, 20.8 minutes with mothers, and 25.8 minutes with fathers (see Figure 1.1).

Activity Diversity. An ANOVA was conducted with three between-subject independent variables of grade, sex, and romantic partner status, and one within-subject independent variable of relationships. Activity diversity was the dependent variable. Main effects emerged for sex, $F(1, 225) = 4.57$, $p < .05$; and for relationships, $F(3, 192) = 12.08$, $p < .001$. There were also two-way interactions between relationships and grade, $F(9, 192) = 3.45$, $p < .001$; and between relationships and sex, $F(3, 192) = 5.51$, $p < .001$. Follow-up ANOVAs, conducted separately for each grade, revealed relationship main effects (p's < .05) for seventh graders, ninth graders, tenth and eleventh graders, and twelfth graders. Paired t-tests indicated that among seventh graders, mothers were involved in the greatest number of different weekly activities; among ninth graders, the scope of different activities was greatest for friends and romantic partners; among tenth, eleventh, and twelfth graders, activity diversity was greatest with romantic partners. Follow-up ANOVAs, conducted separately for each sex, revealed relationship main effects (p's < .001) for males and females. Paired t-tests indicated that males reported the most activity diversity with romantic partners, and females reported the greatest number of different weekly activities with romantic partners and mothers (see Table 1.2).

Figure 1.1. Daily Social Interaction Among Adolescents With and Without Romantic Partners

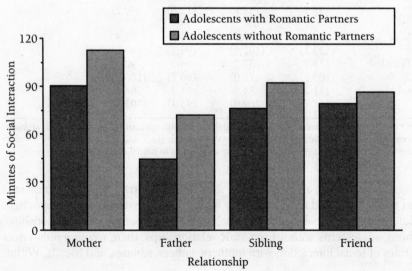

In sum, relationship differences in weekly activity diversity emerged for grade and sex, but not for romantic partner status. Older adolescents and males reported the greatest number of different activities with romantic partners; younger adolescents reported the greatest number of different activities with mothers; females reported the greatest number of different activities with romantic partners and mothers.

Influence Strength. An ANOVA was conducted with three between-subject independent variables of grade, sex, and romantic partner status, and one within-subject independent variable of relationships. Influence strength was the dependent variable. Main effects emerged for grade, $F(3, 202) = 3.32$, $p < .05$; and for relationships, $F(3, 169) = 76.12$, $p < .001$. Tukey's contrasts (p's < .05) indicated that twelfth graders (M = 101.3, SD = 25.3) reported less average relationship influence than seventh graders (M = 120.0, SD = 25.1), with ninth graders (M = 118.6, SD = 24.2) and tenth and eleventh graders (M = 119.5, SD = 26.2) in between. Paired t-tests (p's < .001) indicated that mothers (M = 139.3, SD = 33.5), romantic partners (M = 132.9, SD = 36.5), and fathers (M = 129.2, SD = 38.3) were more influential than friends (M = 104.5, SD = 32.8) and siblings (M = 93.9, SD = 35.7).

To summarize, influence strength differed across relationships and grades but not as a function of sex or romantic partner status. The overall influence

Table 1.2. Weekly Activity Diversity Within Adolescent Relationships

	Relationship				
	Mother M (SD)	Father M (SD)	Sibling M (SD)	Friend M (SD)	Romantic Partner M (SD)
Grade					
7th	9.4ᵃ	6.5ᵇ	7.0ᵇ	6.9ᵇ	7.8ᵇ
	(5.7)	(5.5)	(5.7)	(5.2)	(6.7)
9th	8.8ᵃ	4.9ᶜ	6.1ᵇᶜ	10.1ᵃ	10.6ᵃᵇ
	(5.2)	(3.9)	(5.3)	(6.6)	(4.0)
10th/11th	6.9ᵃᵇ	4.3ᶜ	6.2ᵇᶜ	7.1ᵃᵇ	10.3ᵃ
	(5.1)	(3.2)	(6.1)	(6.0)	(6.0)
12th	6.9ᵇᶜ	4.1ᵈ	6.2ᶜ	7.9ᵇ	11.3ᵃ
	(4.4)	(3.3)	(5.8)	(4.6)	(6.1)
Sex					
Male	6.6ᵇ	5.4ᶜ	6.4ᵇᶜ	7.1ᵇ	10.8ᵃ
	(4.5)	(4.8)	(6.0)	(5.1)	(6.7)
Female	9.4ᵃ	5.1ᵈ	6.7ᶜ	8.1ᵇ	9.5ᵃᵇ
	(5.5)	(4.4)	(5.4)	(5.6)	(5.9)
Total	8.3	5.3	6.5	7.7	10.1
	(5.3)	(4.6)	(5.7)	(5.4)	(6.2)

Note: Comparisons among mothers, fathers, siblings, and friends involved all participants; means and standard deviations for these relationships include 245 adolescents. Comparisons of romantic partners with mothers, fathers, siblings, and friends involved only participants with romantic relationships; means and standard deviations for romantic partners include 118 adolescents. Within each grade and sex (rows), different superscripts denote significant ($p < .05$) relationship differences in paired t-tests.

of relationships with mothers, fathers, siblings, friends, and romantic partners declined across the adolescent years. Subjects consistently rated parents and romantic partners as their most influential relationships, regardless of grade, sex, and romantic partner status.

Interdependent and Close Relationships. Analyses of interdependent relationships included 226 adolescents (19 were eliminated because of missing data on one or more subscales). Analyses of close relationships included 204 adolescents (14 were eliminated because of missing data and 27 were eliminated because someone other than a mother, father, sibling, friend, or romantic partner was selected as the closest relationship). Analyses of measurement concordance included 191 adolescents (54 were eliminated due to a lack of data on the close or interdependent relationship).

Interdependent Relationships. A 5 (relationships) × 4 (grade) chi-square revealed differences in the distribution of interdependent relationships, χ (12) = 61.85, $p < .001$. Relationships with mothers emerged as interdependent for most seventh graders; mothers and friends prevailed for ninth graders; the interdependent relationships of tenth graders were divided among mothers, romantic partners, and friends; and relationships with romantic partners were most likely to be interdependent for twelfth graders (see Table 1.3). A 5 (relationships) × 2 (sex) chi-square revealed differences in the distribution of interdependent relationships, χ (4) = 24.15, $p < .001$. Relationships with mothers emerged as interdependent for most females. A similar proportion of male friends, mothers, romantic partners, and fathers were interdependent (see Table 1.3). There were no statistically significant chi-square differences between adolescents with and without romantic partners in interdependent relationships.

In sum, interdependent relationships differed according to grade and sex, but not according to romantic partner status. Mothers emerged as the interdependent relationship of most younger adolescents and females, romantic partners tended to be the interdependent relationship of older adolescents, and parents and peers were equally represented as the interdependent relationship of males.

Close Relationships. A 5 (relationships) × 4 (grade) chi-square revealed differences in the distribution of close relationships, χ (12) = 42.27, $p < .001$. Mothers were selected by most seventh graders as a close relationship, friends and mothers prevailed during the ninth grade, friends and romantic partners were chosen by most tenth and eleventh graders, and romantic partners were identified most frequently as the closest relationship of twelfth graders (see Table 1.3). There were no statistically significant chi-square differences in the close relationships of males and females; neither were there differences between adolescents with and without romantic partners.

To summarize, close relationships differed across grades, but not as a function of sex or romantic partner status. Younger adolescents tended to identify mothers as their closest relationship, whereas older adolescents were most likely to name romantic partners.

Table 1.3. Interdependent and Close Adolescent Relationships

	Relationship				
	Mother n (Row percent)	Father n (Row percent)	Sibling n (Row percent)	Friend n (Row percent)	Romantic Partner n (Row percent)
Interdependent Relationships					
Grade					
7th	55 (55)	16 (16)	13 (13)	11 (11)	5 (5)
9th	15 (47)	3 (9)	2 (6)	11 (34)	1 (3)
10th/11th	8 (33)	2 (8)	2 (8)	6 (25)	6 (25)
12th	15 (21)	3 (4)	7 (10)	16 (23)	29 (41)
Sex					
Male	23 (25)	18 (20)	10 (11)	23 (25)	18 (20)
Female	70 (52)	6 (4)	14 (10)	21 (16)	23 (17)
Total	93 (41)	24 (11)	24 (11)	44 (19)	41 (18)
Close Relationships					
Grade					
7th	34 (39)	7 (8)	15 (17)	20 (23)	10 (12)
9th	10 (38)	0 (0)	0 (0)	11 (42)	5 (19)
10th/11th	4 (15)	0 (0)	3 (11)	10 (37)	10 (37)
12th	8 (12)	4 (6)	8 (12)	16 (25)	29 (45)
Total	56 (27)	11 (5)	26 (13)	57 (28)	54 (26)

Note: For each participant ($n = 226$), an interdependent relationship represents the relationship with the greatest composite score on the interaction frequency, activity diversity, and influence strength scales. For each participant ($n = 204$), a close relationship represents the self-reported closest relationship.

Measurement Concordance. Parents were more apt to be rated as interdependent than as close, whereas there was a greater tendency for peer relationships to be a close but not interdependent. A similar number of participants scored siblings as close and interdependent (see Table 1.3).

There was 45.6 percent agreement between measures of interdependent relationships and reports of close relationships. The proportion of interdependent relationships identified as close ranged from 20 percent with fathers to 72 percent with romantic partners. Disagreement between indices varied with relationships: adolescents with fathers and siblings as interdependent relationships tended to identify mothers as close relationships, adolescents with mothers and romantic partners as interdependent relationships named friends as close relationships, and adolescents with friends as interdependent relationships labeled romantic partners as close relationships (see Table 1.4). Three separate chi-square analyses failed to find statistically significant differences in the distribution of concordance rates as a function of romantic partner status, grade, and sex.

In sum, less than half of the adolescents rated the same relationship close and interdependent, a trend that did not vary with grade, sex, or romantic

Table 1.4. Concordance Between Measures of Interdependent and Close Relationships

	Close Relationship				
	Mother n (Row percent)	Father n (Row percent)	Sibling n (Row percent)	Friend n (Row percent)	Romantic Partner n (Row percent)
Interdependent Relationship					
Mother	33 (43)	3 (4)	6 (8)	25 (32)	10 (13)
Father	9 (45)	4 (20)	3 (15)	3 (15)	1 (5)
Sibling	6 (32)	0 (0)	8 (42)	3 (16)	2 (11)
Friend	4 (11)	0 (0)	8 (22)	14 (39)	10 (28)
Romantic Partner	1 (3)	3 (8)	1 (3)	6 (15)	28 (72)

Note: An interdependent relationship represents the relationship with the greatest composite score on the interaction frequency, activity diversity, and influence strength scales. A close relationship represents the self-reported closest relationship. Concordance scores include only those participants ($n = 191$) reporting interdependent and close relationships with mothers, fathers, siblings, friends, or romantic partners.

partner status. Peers were apt to be close, and family members (especially mothers) tended to be interdependent. Concordance was greatest for romantic partners, indicating that most interdependent romantic relationships were also perceived as close.

Discussion

Reports from 245 eleven- to nineteen-year-olds, delineating interconnections in adolescent close relationships, addressed three questions:

1. *Do relationship interdependence and closeness differ across adolescence?* Overall, interdependence and closeness appeared to shift from family members to peers. Specifically, younger adolescents rated mothers as close and interdependent, whereas older adolescents scored romantic partners as close and interdependent. Developmental alterations in specific interconnections, however, were not uniform. Activity diversity and interaction frequency declined with parents, increased with romantic partners, and peaked at mid-adolescence with friends. That adolescents spend less time with family members and more time with age-mates is well documented (Larson and Richards, 1991; Montemayor and Brownlee, 1987), but the results of the present study are among the first indications that these changes extend to the number of different social activities. The patterns are consistent with the premise that as constraints on voluntary relationships are lifted, adolescents widen connections with peers and curtail them with family members (Laursen, 1996). They also lend credence to assertions that adolescents prefer the reciprocity-based exchanges of horizontal relationships to the authority-based exchanges of vertical relationships (Youniss, 1980). Influence strength provides an intriguing contrast to measures of companionship. Total influence in all relationships

declined across adolescence, yet relative influence did not differ: mothers, romantic partners, and fathers were more influential than friends and siblings at each grade level. The findings, added to an already differentiated picture of control, conformity, and relative power during adolescence (see Collins and Repinski, 1994, for review), indicate that developmental shifts in companionship and closeness favoring voluntary and horizontal relationships over involuntary and vertical relationships are not accompanied by analogous developmental shifts in influence.

2. *Do adolescents with romantic partners report less interdependence and closeness with family members and friends than adolescents without romantic partners?* The effects of romantic relationships appear to be relative rather than absolute. Direct comparisons of family and friend relationships reveal more similarities than differences among adolescents with and without romantic partners. Romantic relationships were not associated with differences in closeness and interdependence with mothers, fathers, siblings, and friends, except insofar as they were linked to interaction frequency. Apparently adolescents with romantic partners maintain activities, influence, and closeness with friends and family members, but sacrifice time devoted to each in order to accommodate romantic relationships. These findings suggest that family and friend relationships are largely unaffected by participation in romantic relationships.

Yet when romantic relationships are considered from the wider perspective of relative closeness and interdependence, clear differences emerge between adolescents with and without romantic partners. Participation in romantic relationships more than doubled across adolescence, dramatically revising the calculus of close relationships: adolescents with romantic partners are obviously more likely than those without romantic partners to indicate that these relationships are close, interdependent, and influential, and that they contain substantial amounts of social interaction and shared activities. As adolescents grow older, romantic relationships are increasingly apt to lead all relationships in characteristics reflecting interdependence and closeness. Thus, romantic relationships are probably more important for what they represent than for any of the specific changes they may produce in other relationships. Romantic relationships appear to alter the dynamics of adolescent communal relationships in that they represent a new type of voluntary, horizontal relationship that combines influence with closeness and companionship. Seen in this light, romantic relationships emerge as the first truly interdependent peer relationship at a time of waning interdependence with parents.

3. *Are relationships with the greatest levels of interdependence perceived to be the closest relationships?* The results indicate that adolescents do not view closeness to be synonymous with an objectively defined measure of interdependence; the same relationship emerged as close and interdependent in less than half of individual accounts. Close relationships tended to be horizontal and voluntary, whereas interdependent relationships were often vertical and involuntary. These results could be interpreted as support for the contention that

interdependence is distinct from affective experience (Berscheid, Snyder, and Omoto, 1989a, 1989b). Or perhaps closeness and interdependence are relationship-specific constructs, with the former emphasizing the salient aspects of peer affiliations and the latter capturing the defining features of parent-child relationships. Another possibility, however, is that interdependence and closeness are similar but subjective reports of closeness have a greater tendency to reflect socially desirable responses than behaviorally oriented measures of interdependence. Peer culture in Western society demands fealty towards age-mates at the expense of adults (Bronfenbrenner, 1972; Coleman, 1961), which may prompt adolescents to overreport closeness with peers and underreport it with parents.

These results prompt a final question: *Is interdependence relevant to adolescent relationships?* We can only speculate, of course, but interdependence appears to be a critical mechanism underlying distinctions between voluntary and involuntary relationships, perhaps providing an impetus for developmental shifts in social exchange within these relationships. Similarities between these results and reports of social support (Furman and Buhrmester, 1992) and affective experience (Larson and Richards, 1991) suggest that this measure of interdependence accurately reflects the changing dynamics of close relationships across adolescence. Furthermore, alterations in interdependence capture developmental distinctions between horizontal and vertical relationships such that changes in parent and peer reciprocity (Hunter and Youniss, 1982) mirror changes in social interaction, activity diversity, and influence. Beyond these parallels, interdependence reflects subtle nuances in relationship interconnections. For instance, changes in perceived closeness appear to precede changes in different aspects of interdependence. Parent-adolescent interdependence may persist because influence does not ebb from involuntary relationships at the same rate that companionship and closeness do. It follows that interdependence may lag behind closeness in voluntary relationships because companionship and closeness do not automatically translate into influence.

We conclude that social exchange theory (Kelley and Thibaut, 1978) extends models of adolescent development by elaborating behavioral mechanisms of relationship change. Cognitive maturity and increased autonomy provide adolescents with opportunities to explore social exchanges with friends and romantic partners, which in turn alters perceptions of and behavior within parent-child relationships (Laursen, 1996). Interconnections with peers widen as interdependence deepens, prompting a gradual shift in the peer social world to encompass romantic partners as well as friends. Although parental and cultural constraints limit romantic social exchanges during early adolescence, age and maturity afford late adolescents greater experience with the resources and benefits associated with romantic relationships (Laursen and Jensen-Campbell, in press). Relationships with romantic partners gradually evolve into the primary source of love, support, and interdependence for adolescents; escalating interconnections require constant revision of social exchanges and, by the end of the adolescent years, romantic relationships increasingly resemble those of young adults. Thus, interdependence may be a mechanism that prompts the realignment of social exchanges in adolescent relationships.

This study is not without shortcomings and should be considered exploratory. Sample sizes were uneven, drawn from study halls in rural North America. Although there is little reason to suspect that the sample and distribution of participants systematically altered relationship results, the findings require replication before they can be generalized to adolescents in other settings.

In closing, fundamental relationship shifts in adolescent interdependence and closeness occur as voluntary and horizontal relationships gradually supersede involuntary and vertical relationships. The increasing incidence of romantic partners does not appear to change specific interconnections in other adolescent relationships (aside from reducing the amount of time spent together) so much as it realigns relative relationship closeness and interdependence. Age-related manifestations of adolescent interdependence differ; influence is reserved for parents and romantic partners, whereas activities and social interaction expand in peer relationships and contract in family relationships.

References

Argyle, M., and Furnham, A. "Sources of Satisfaction and Conflict in Long-Term Relationships." *Journal of Marriage and the Family,* 1983, *45,* 481–493.

Berscheid, E. "Interpersonal Attraction." In G. Lindzey and E. Aronson (eds.), *Handbook of Social Psychology.* Hillsdale, N.J.: Erlbaum, 1985.

Berscheid, E., Snyder, M., and Omoto, A. M. "Issues in Studying Close Relationships: Conceptualizing and Measuring Closeness." In C. Hendrick (ed.), *Review of Personality and Social Psychology,* Vol. 10: *Close Relationships.* Thousand Oaks, Calif.: Sage, 1989a.

Berscheid, E., Snyder, M., and Omoto, A. M. "The Relationship Closeness Inventory: Assessing the Closeness of Interpersonal Relationships." *Journal of Personality and Social Psychology,* 1989b, *57,* 792–807.

Bronfenbrenner, U. *Two Worlds of Childhood: U.S. and U.S.S.R.* Thousand Oaks, Calif.: Sage, 1972.

Brown, B. B. "You're Going Out with Whom?! Peer Group Influences on Adolescent Romantic Relationships." In W. Furman, B. B. Brown, and C. Feiring (eds.), *Contemporary Perspectives on Adolescent Romantic Relationships.* New York: Cambridge University Press, in press.

Clark, M. S., and Mills, J. "Interpersonal Attraction in Exchange and Communal Relationships." *Journal of Personality and Social Psychology,* 1979, *37,* 12–24.

Clark, M. S., and Reis, H. T. "Interpersonal Processes in Close Relationships." *Annual Review of Psychology,* 1988, *39,* 609–672.

Clark-Lempers, D. S., Lempers, J. D., and Ho, C. "Early, Middle, and Late Adolescents' Perceptions of Their Relationships with Significant Others." *Journal of Adolescent Research,* 1991, *6,* 296–315.

Coleman, J. S. *The Adolescent Society.* New York: Free Press, 1961.

Collins, W. A., and Repinski, D. J. "Relationships During Adolescence: Continuity and Change in Interpersonal Perspective." In R. Montemayor, G. R. Adams, and T. P. Gullotta (eds.), *Personal Relationships During Adolescence.* Thousand Oaks, Calif.: Sage, 1994.

Foa, U. G. "Interpersonal and Economic Resources." *Science,* 1973, *171,* 345–351.

Furman, W., and Buhrmester, D. "Age and Sex Differences in Perceptions of Networks of Personal Relationships." *Child Development,* 1992, *63,* 103–115.

Graziano, W. G. "A Developmental Approach to Social Exchange Processes." In J. C. Masters and K. Yarkin-Levin (eds.), *Boundary Areas in Social and Developmental Psychology.* Orlando: Academic Press, 1984.

Graziano, W. G., Musser, L. M., Rosen, S., and Shaffer, D. "The Development of Fair-Play Standards in Same- and Mixed-Race Situations: Three Converging Studies." *Child Development,* 1984, *53,* 938–947.

Hartup, W. W., and Laursen, B. "Relationships as Developmental Contexts." In R. Cohen and A. W. Siegel (eds.), *Context and Development.* Hillsdale, N.J.: Erlbaum, 1991.

Hunter, F. T., and Youniss, J. "Changes in Functions of Three Relations During Adolescence." *Developmental Psychology,* 1982, *18,* 806–811.

Kelley, H. H., Berscheid, E., Christensen, A., Harvey, J. H., Huston, T. L., Levinger, G., McClintock, E., Peplau, L. A., and Peterson, D. R. *Close Relationships.* New York: Freeman, 1983.

Kelley, H. H., and Thibaut, J. W. *Interpersonal Relations: A Theory of Interdependence.* New York: Wiley, 1978.

Larson, R., and Richards, M. H. "Daily Companionship in Late Childhood and Early Adolescence: Changing Developmental Contexts." *Child Development,* 1991, *62,* 284–300.

Laursen, B. "Closeness and Conflict in Adolescent Peer Relationships: Interdependence with Friends and Romantic Partners." In W. M. Bukowski, A. F. Newcomb, and W. W. Hartup (eds.), *The Company They Keep: Friendships in Childhood and Adolescence.* New York: Cambridge University Press, 1996.

Laursen, B., and Jensen-Campbell, L. A. "The Nature and Functions of Social Exchange in Adolescent Romantic Relationships." In W. Furman, B. B. Brown, and C. Feiring (eds.), *Contemporary Perspectives on Adolescent Romantic Relationships.* New York: Cambridge University Press, in press.

Montemayor, R., and Brownlee, J. R. "Fathers, Mothers, and Adolescents: Gender-Based Differences in Parental Roles During Adolescence." *Journal of Youth and Adolescence,* 1987, *16,* 281–291.

Repinski, D. J. "Adolescents' Close Relationships with Parents and Friends." Unpublished doctoral dissertation, Institute of Child Development, University of Minnesota, 1993.

Rubin, Z. *Liking and Loving: An Invitation to Social Psychology.* Austin, Tex.: Holt, Rinehart and Winston, 1973.

Wilder, D. "Age-Related Changes in Relationship Closeness, Authority, and Reciprocity During Adolescence." Unpublished master's thesis, Department of Psychology, Florida Atlantic University, 1995.

Youniss, J. *Parents and Peers in Social Development: A Piaget-Sullivan Perspective.* Chicago: University of Chicago Press, 1980.

BRETT LAURSEN *is associate professor of psychology and chair of the Division of Science, College of Liberal Arts, Florida Atlantic University.*

VICKIE A. WILLIAMS *is a doctoral candidate in the Department of Psychology at Florida Atlantic University*

A framework for examining developmental changes in romantic relationships is presented. The chapter describes research illustrating these developmental differences and delineates an agenda for subsequent developmental work.

Adolescent Romantic Relationships: A Developmental Perspective

Wyndol Furman, Elizabeth A. Wehner

If we were to look back at our romantic experiences, most of us would be struck by the changes that have occurred in our relationships. Our early forays could usually be characterized as superficial or awkward, yet quite important to us at the time. Over the course of adolescence and adulthood, we gained further experience and learned ways of interacting. Typically relationships became more "serious" and lasted longer. At some point many, though not all, of us became involved in a long-term, committed relationship, such as a marriage.

Although it is clear that romantic relationships typically undergo many changes over the course of development, social scientists have yet to delineate the precise nature of such changes. Most of the empirical work has focused on romantic relationships in the college years or adulthood, and relatively few studies have examined romantic relationships in adolescence. Almost no work has considered age differences in these relationships. As a consequence, we have little scientific data on the developmental course of romantic relationships.

In the present chapter, we present a theoretical framework that considers some of the developmental changes in these relationships. We describe several empirical studies that have examined age differences, and conclude by outlining an agenda for subsequent work. Although we focus on age-related changes in romantic relationships, we also discuss some of the changes that occur over the course of particular relationships.

Preparation of this chapter was supported by Grant 50106 from the National Institute of Mental Health. The first study presented was done in collaboration with Duane Buhrmester. Appreciation is expressed to German Posado, Valerie Simon, and Everett Waters for their stimulating comments on topics addressed herein.

We describe changes that commonly occur over the course of development, but it is important to emphasize at the outset that there is not a single path of romantic development. Romantic relationships are quite diverse in nature, both across and within cultures (Dion and Dion, 1996). The timing and intensity of romantic involvement varies. During adolescence, some individuals are more interested in romantic relationships than others and are further along the developmental pathway they are taking. The sequence of dating experiences is also far from fixed and is often influenced by chance meetings and events. We suspect that some adolescents are more likely than others to get involved in a long-term relationship, but such involvement also depends on whether one happens to have met the "right person." Finally, there is not a single endpoint or aim. Many individuals get married or develop a long-term committed relationship, but others do not. The line from the children's song, "First comes love, then comes marriage, then comes Junior in a baby carriage," may apply in some instances, but not in others. Thus the descriptions of developmental changes that are presented here are not intended as universals, but they are believed to be common age-related changes and can thus shed light on the social processes involved in these relationships.

This chapter principally discusses developmental changes in heterosexual relationships. Many of the ideas are expected to be applicable to homosexual relationships, but some important differences can be expected as well. For example, passionate friendships—platonic yet intense relationships—may be more likely to play an important role in the romantic development of lesbian, bisexual, and gay youth than in the romantic development of heterosexual youth (see Diamond, Savin-Williams, and Dube, in press).

A Behavioral Systems Conceptualization

In an attempt to integrate the insights of attachment and neo-Sullivanian theories, we developed a behavioral systems conceptualization of romantic relationships (Furman and Wehner, 1994). In particular, we proposed that a romantic partner can become a major figure in the functioning of the attachment, caregiving, affiliative, and sexual behavioral systems. That is, the partner may serve as an attachment figure, who is sought out at times of distress; conversely, the individual may provide similar support, comfort, and caregiving to the partner. The person may turn to the partner for companionship and friendship, as romantic relationships provide rich opportunities for cooperation, mutualism, reciprocal altruism, and the co-construction of a relationship (Furman, in press). Finally, the individual may turn to the partner for sexual fulfillment.

Of course most of these functions are not necessarily met in romantic relationships. Adolescents have other individuals in their social networks who can serve as attachment figures, affiliative partners, or individuals to whom they provide care. These individuals are organized into a hierarchy according to their importance to the adolescent. A romantic partner is expected to become part of this hierarchy of figures and gradually move up in importance in the hierarchy as the relationship develops. For example, an individual may be less likely to seek out a partner when distressed early on in the development of a relationship than later when the relationship is more established and the level of trust is typically greater. Such changes are expected to occur not only within the course of a particular relationship but also over the course of a series of relationships. Thus, as individuals grow older and acquire more experience in various romantic relationships, they may be more likely to turn to a partner to fulfill these functions than when they were younger and less experienced (with some notable exceptions, described subsequently).

One of the reasons that age changes are expected to occur in the hierarchy of figures is that adolescents and young adults are learning how to interact with romantic partners. As an individual learns how to use a partner as an attachment, caregiving, affiliative, or sexual figure, he or she is likely to do so more frequently and more skillfully (once again, with some notable exceptions). Some of what one learns is expected to carry over to later relationships, thus making it easier to turn to subsequent partners. After all, most adults feel more comfortable and able in a romantic context than they did when they were younger.

Changes with age and experience are expected to be particularly striking during adolescence. Prior to adolescence, most children have relatively limited contact with other-sex peers because children's play occurs primarily in sex-segregated groups (Maccoby, 1988). As a consequence of such gender segregation, boys and girls develop different means of playing and exerting influence (Maccoby, 1990). With the onset of adolescence, children become interested in the other sex, but they face several challenges. They have to determine what kind of relationship they want—a romantic relationship or friendship. The former is a completely new kind of relationship, but even in the case of the latter they have to interact with a person who is likely to have a different style of interacting because of the earlier gender segregation. Moreover, they need to address the sexual desires they are feeling. Lesbian, gay, and bisexual youth face the additional challenge of determining who they are attracted to. Finally, they need to consider their peers' reactions to their behavior because their status in the peer group may be influenced by whether they have a romantic relationship and whether it is with the right person. Needless to say, these are complex tasks, and the early interactions or relationships are awkward experiments.

In their early relationships, adolescents are not very concerned with the fulfillment of attachment or caregiving needs or even sexual or affiliative needs. Instead, their focus is on who they are, how attractive they are, how they should interact with someone, and how it all looks to their peer group (see Brown, in press, for a similar account). Some affiliative and sexual behavior occurs, but early on adolescents are primarily learning how to affiliate with the other sex, how to engage in sexual activity, and which sexual activities to engage in. Only after the adolescent has acquired some basic competencies in interacting with the other sex does the fulfillment of affiliative and sexual needs become a central function of these relationships. During middle adolescence, the majority of adolescents in the United States have at least one exclusive relationship, lasting for several months to perhaps a year (Feiring, 1996; Thornton, 1990). In middle adolescence, they also become less concerned with their peer status and the status value of the partner, although such considerations are still important for many individuals (Brown, Eicher, and Petrie, 1986; Dunphy, 1963; Gavin and Furman, 1989).

The attachment and caregiving systems are expected to become more significant in relationships in late adolescence and adulthood, as relationships with parents undergo transformations and the press to find a new primary attachment figure increases. In fact, extensive caregiving and fully developed attachments usually do not occur except in relatively long-term relationships. Even in long-term relationships, a romantic partner is expected to serve as a sexual figure and as an affiliative figure before becoming an attachment figure or a recipient of caregiving. Thus a romantic partner usually does not become a significant figure for all four behavioral systems until a relatively long relationship develops in late adolescence or early adulthood.

Consistent with these ideas, proximity seeking, which we consider affiliative behavior, emerges earlier in relationships than safe haven or secure base behavior (Hazan and Zeifman, 1994). Proximity seeking also emerges in romantic and peer relationships at an earlier age than either safe haven or secure base behavior. Similarly, fifteen-year-olds emphasize affiliative features when asked to list advantages of having a romantic partner, but eighteen-year-olds begin to discuss attachment elements as well (Feiring, 1993).

Age Differences in Social Support. The proposition that romantic partners would move up in the hierarchy of figures with age was supported in our earlier research on children's and adolescents' social networks (Furman and Buhrmester, 1992). In that study, 549 youth in the fourth grade, seventh grade, tenth grade, and college completed Network of Relationship Inventories, which assessed their perceptions of their relationships with parents, siblings, grandparents, same-sex friends, and romantic partners. For each relationship, they rated seven types of support they received: companionship, intimacy, instrumental help, affection, enhancement of worth, nurturance of the other, and reliable alliance—a sense of a lasting bond. A measure of overall support was derived by averaging the seven types.

The increasing importance of romantic relationships was apparent in several ways. The proportion of individuals who stated that they had a boyfriend or girlfriend generally increased with age (fourth grade, 46 percent; seventh grade, 36 percent; tenth grade, 45 percent; college, 67 percent). The number of fourth graders claiming to have such a relationship is surprisingly high, but examination of the overall support ratings suggests that a number of these relationships may have been in name only. As shown in Figure 2.1, ratings of overall support were low in the fourth grade, and showed a significant increase over the four grades, $F(3,380) = 6.60, p < .01$.

Figure 2.1. Mean Ratings of Support for Each Relationship Type at Each Grade Level

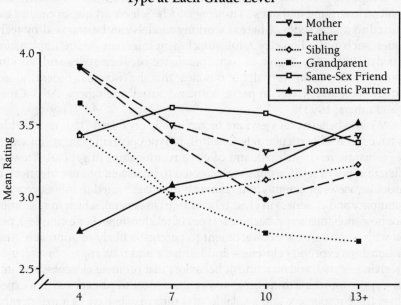

Figure 2.1 also illustrates that changes occurred in the amount of support in romantic relationships relative to that in other significant relationships in the network. In the fourth grade, romantic partners were ranked sixth in terms of the amount of overall support. In the seventh grade, they were tied for fourth with siblings and grandparents. In the tenth grade, they were tied for second with mothers. In college, men rated their partners as the most supportive individual in the network, whereas women gave equally high ratings to their partners, mothers, same-sex friends, and siblings.

Views of Romantic Relationships. Developmental changes are also expected in adolescents' views of romantic relationships. By views we mean perceptions of romantic relationships, of the self in relationships, and of partners (Furman and Simon, in press; Furman and Wehner, 1994). Our concept of views stems from the ideas of working models and attachment styles in attachment theory (Bowlby, 1973; Main, Kaplan, and Cassidy, 1985), but is intended to be more general in application. That is, we believe that the basic concepts of working models and styles can be applied to other close relationships that are not attachment relationships, such as most friendships and adolescent romantic relationships. In other words, we conceptualize views as representations of relationships, not just as the attachment processes in these relationships.

Our conceptualization of views is intended to incorporate both conscious and unconscious, internal representations of relationships. Many of our ideas apply to both levels of representations, but we also distinguish between these two components of views. We refer to conscious representations as *styles,* and to unconscious, internal ones as *working models.* Self-report questionnaires can be used to assess styles, whereas working models can be assessed by techniques, such as the Berkeley Adult Attachment Interview (Main, Caplan, and Cassidy, 1985). The degree of correspondence between styles and working models remains controversial, but it is clear that the two are not identical (see Bartholomew and Shaver, in press; Borman-Spurrell and others, 1993; Crowell and others, 1993).

We also believe that views are hierarchically organized. That is, individuals have views of particular relationships, of types of relationships (for example, romantic relationships), and of close relationships in general. Views of different types of relationships are expected to be related but not identical. In particular, views of parent-child relationships are expected to influence views of intimacy and closeness in close relationships in general, which in turn influence how individuals approach new types of relationships. For example, a person with a secure view of attachment to parents is likely to approach other relationships expecting closeness and intimacy, and thus engage in affiliative, caregiving, sexual, and attachment behaviors that promote closeness and intimacy. A person with a dismissing view of attachment to parents may not expect others to be responsive and available, and thus may behave in a manner that results in some distance. A person with a preoccupied view may be disappointed and frustrated with the intimacy and closeness, and approach other relationships with similar expectations. By the same token, experiences with peers and views of peer relationships should also affect views about close relationships in general, particularly with regard to expectations about reciprocity, mutuality, and other affiliation-related features

At the same time, romantic views are not expected to be identical to views of parent-child relationships and friendships, because experiences in romantic relationships are expected to play a particularly important role in shaping views of these relationships. After all, to be effective, views should be open to changes that reflect experience. Adolescents may approach romantic relationships on the basis of their experiences in other close relationships, but if their experiences differ enough from existing expectations, romantic views would be expected to develop differently. The possibility that the experiences could be different is not remote either, as the partner as well the adolescent influences the interactions that occur, and the two commonly enter these relationships with different views (see Furman and Flanagan, 1997).

Age Differences in Romantic Views. The present emphasis on the role of experience implies that views may show changes as adolescents' romantic lives unfold. Romantic views may become more secure, remain consistent, or become less secure. For instance, individuals may develop more secure views of their romantic relationships if they become more able to fulfill attachment, caregiving, or affiliative needs in these relationships. A particularly supportive partner in a long-term relationship may foster secure views as well. Conversely, insecure individuals may consciously or unconsciously recreate the insecure relationships they expect. For example, dismissing individuals may act in ways that discourage intimacy or closeness, and thus may reinforce their dismissing views. Preoccupied individuals' controlling, dependent, or overly involving behavior may lead to being rebuffed by their partners. Thus these individuals may become more skillful, but more skillful in developing the relationships they have come to expect. Finally, views may become less secure as a result of deleterious relationships or experiences, such as infidelity by a trusted partner, sexual assault, or physical abuse.

Some data suggest that views are likely to become more secure rather than more insecure. In particular, we compared the views of high school and college women, using a sample of 243 students who were predominantly Caucasian and middle-class (Furman and Wehner, 1993). We also examined the effects of romantic relationship status by dividing each age group into those who were casually dating and those who were seeing someone exclusively (going "steady" or having a serious relationship). A small number of individuals who had never dated or who were engaged, living with someone, or married were excluded from these analyses.

The samples were administered the Behavioral Systems Questionnaire to assess relational styles with romantic partners, mothers, fathers, and close friends. The measure assessed perceptions of attachment, care received, and affiliation in each of the four types of relationships; perceptions of sexuality in romantic relationships and care provided to friends and romantic partners were also assessed. Secure, dismissing, and preoccupied styles or conscious views were assessed for each behavioral system in each type of relationship (see Furman and Simon, in press; Wehner, 1992). For example, an item on the secure attachment scale was "I consistently turn to ——— when upset or worried," whereas a preoccupied affiliation item was "I want to do more things with ——— than they want to."

The corresponding attachment, care received, and affiliative scales for each of the three styles were correlated with one another in each of the four relationships (mean $r = .37$). These correlations suggest that representations of different systems are coordinated or integrated such that they can be conceptualized as *relational styles*. Accordingly, general relational scores for secure, preoccupied, and dismissing styles were calculated by standardizing and averaging the scores for the three different behavioral systems measured in each of the four types of relationships.

The stylistic scores for all relationships were subjected to two-way analyses of variance in which age and relationship status were factors. Table 2.1 presents the mean scores for each group. College women were less preoccupied and less dismissing than high school women, $F(1, 164)$'s = 7.97 and 4.96, respectively, p's < .05. Interestingly, the mean scores of the two age groups on the secure style variable were essentially identical. If this differential pattern of age differences on the secure and insecure variables can be replicated, it would suggest that the experiences incurred with age may lead individuals to feel less

Table 2.1. Mean Ratings of Relational Styles by Age and Dating Status

	High School		College	
	Casual	Exclusive	Casual	Exclusive
Romantic Partners				
Secure[R]	−.26	.49	−.21	.40
Dismissing[A,R]	.26	−.25	.07	−.55
Preoccupied[A,R]	.17	−.03	−.04	−.56
Mother				
Secure	.06	−.10	.15	.01
Dismissing[A, AxR]	.05	.19	−.05	−.50
Preoccupied[A]	−.02	.20	−.21	−.27
Father				
Secure	.09	−.17	.24	.19
Dismissing[A]	−.05	.12	−.18	−.20
Preoccupied[A, AxR]	−.09	.25	−.07	−.53
Friend				
Secure[AxR]	.12	.21	.24	−.26
Dismissing	−.00	.03	−.06	−.06
Preoccupied	.05	−.04	−.21	−.23

Note: Superscripts by variable indicate significant effects, $p < .05$. A = age, R = relationship status,

insecure in their perceptions of romantic relationships, but the perceptions of security may not increase except as a particular relationship develops. For example, individuals may learn not to be dismissing of attachment needs or overly preoccupied with romantic partners' availability and investment, but they may not be more likely to perceive them as individuals to turn to unless they have such a relationship. Alternatively, the results may simply not be fully consistent across the secure and insecure scales; after all, a decrease in insecurity would seem to imply an increase in security. In either case, it is important to note that we do not interpret the findings as suggesting that individuals start with insecure views of romantic relationships. The Behavioral Systems Questionnaire assesses security on a continuum. Subjects in the high school and college sample were also administered Hazan and Shaver's (1987) categorical measure of attachment style; 47 percent of the high school girls reported having a secure style, as did 52 percent of the college girls. Thus we believe that one's initial views of romantic relationships may stem from the views and experiences in other relationships and may be either secure or insecure. The present results simply suggest that *on average* romantic styles tend to become more secure or less insecure with age.

The analyses of the romantic style scores also revealed effects of relationship status. Women in exclusive relationships were more secure and less preoccupied and dismissing in their romantic styles than those dating more casually, $F(1, 164)$'s = 15.58, 6.02, and 24.85, respectively, p's < .05. Such differences could either stem from the effects of the relationship experience on relational styles or reflect differences between individuals who establish longer relationships and those who do not.

Analyses were also conducted on the stylistic scores for the other types of relationships (see Table 2.1). Compared to the high school women, college women were less preoccupied and less dismissing in their stylistic views of their relationships with mothers, $F(1, 164)$'s = 7.25 and 15.16, respectively, p's < .05. The age difference in the dismissing scores, however, primarily occurred among those who had exclusive relationships, $F(1, 164) = 8.31$, $p < .01$. Similar age differences were found in the scores for father, $F(1, 164)$'s = 6.42 and 4.24, respectively, p's < .05, although here the interaction was for the preoccupied scores, $F(1, 164)$'s = 10.18, $p < .01$. The secure scores did not differ significantly, but the means tended to be higher in the college sample. These findings are consistent with prior work that has found increases in perceptions of support and decreases in perceptions of conflict in parent-child relationships from high school to college (Furman and Buhrmester, 1992; Shaver, Furman, and Buhrmester, 1985).

As to friendship styles, a significant interaction between age and relationship status was found, $F(1, 164) = 6.26$, $p < .05$. College women who had an exclusive dating relationship had less secure views than college women who did not or than high school women, regardless of their romantic status. This pattern suggests that by college, serious romantic relationships may begin to replace close friendships as a source of caregiving, affiliation, and attachment. Apparently the move from home may have a positive effect on family relationships, but either the loss of old friendships or the increased interest in romantic relationships may alter women's perceptions of friendships.

The high school students also completed a Dating History Questionnaire and the Network of Relationships Inventory described previously. Secure romantic style scores were related to satisfaction with dating, $r = .46$, $p < .01$, whereas preoccupied and dismissing scores were negatively related, r's = −.31 and −.18, respectively, p's < .05. Similarly, secure styles were positively correlated with perceptions of supportiveness by their romantic partners, $r = .49$, $p < .05$, and preoccupied and dismissing scores were negatively correlated, r's = −.22 and −.42, respectively, p's < .05.

These analyses examined overt relational styles and not internal working models of the different types of relationships (see Furman and Wehner, 1994). Internal working models may be less likely to be changed by relationship experiences and less influenced by the current nature of a romantic relationship. Some initial data, however, suggests that models, as well as styles, may be related to romantic experiences.

In particular, we examined working models of romantic relationships in a portion of the high school sample. Fifty-four women were administered a Romantic Relationship Interview that was analogous to the Berkeley Adult Attachment Interview. Using Kobak's (1993) Q-sort methodology, multiple coders read transcripts of each interview and sorted seventy-two descriptors into nine categories ranging from very characteristic to very uncharacteristic.

The descriptors focused on interview discourse and attachment-related features of the relationships. The Q-sorts were then correlated with Kobak's prototypic sorts to yield a rating of security. Just as with secure romantic style scores, the security of romantic working models was related to satisfaction with dating, $r = .40$, $p < .05$, and to perceptions of supportiveness by their romantic partners, $r = .34$, $p < .05$. Those who were in exclusive romantic relationships tended to be more secure, but the difference was not significant. Unfortunately, we were not able to administer similar interviews to the college students, and thus were not able to examine age differences in working models of relationships.

Links Across Relationships. Developmental changes may also occur in the *centrality* of constructs—that is, in the pattern of interrelations of variables (Connell and Furman, 1984). As part of our developmental conceptualization, we hypothesized that the quality of romantic relationships is influenced not only by experiences in romantic relationships but also by relationships with friends and parents. In middle adolescence, most romantic partners are expected to be affiliative and sexual figures rather than attachment and caregiving figures. Accordingly, the experiences in romantic relationships and the participants' views of these relationships may be more related to those of friendships than to those of relationships with parents. As the attachment and caregiving system become more important in romantic relationships in late adolescence or adulthood, the links with relationships with parents may become more evident.

Our previously described study on relational styles provides support for these ideas. Parallel versions of the Behavioral Systems Questionnaire were administered to assess relational styles with romantic partners, friends, mothers, and fathers. In the high school sample, all of the corresponding styles with friends and romantic partners were found to be moderately related, $m\ r = .33$. The links between parent-adolescent relationships and romantic relationships were less apparent, $m\ r = .10$, with only two of the six correlations between corresponding styles significant. Parent-adolescent styles were, however, related to corresponding styles of friendship, $m\ r = .22$.

In the college sample, all of the representations of romantic relationships were again related to corresponding ones for friendships, $m\ r = .37$, but unlike the high school sample they were also related to corresponding representations of parent-adolescent relationships in four of six instances, $m\ r = .26$. Corresponding style scores for parents and friends were also related, $m\ r = .26$.

As yet, no single study has compared the correlates of working models at two ages, but it is possible to compare the results of two different studies that have examined links across working models of different relationships. In our study of high school students, those who were interviewed about their romantic relationships were also interviewed about their friendships using an analogous interview, and about their relationships with parents using the Berkeley Adult Attachment Interview. These interviews were also transcribed and coded using Kobak's Q-sort methodology. The pattern of correlations among the security of working model scores for the three relationships resembled that found with our stylistic measures. Ratings of security of working models of romantic relationships were significantly related to ratings of friendships, $r = .47$, $p < .01$, but only tended to be related to ratings of relationships with parents, $r = .26$, n.s. Ratings of friendships and relationships with parents were significantly related, $r = .34$, $p < .01$. In a sample of college students, however, security of models of romantic relationships was related to security of parent-child models and tended to be related to security of models of friendship (kappas $= .42$ and .32). Security of models of friendship and parent-child relationships were also related (kappa $= .57$) (Treboux, Crowell, Owens, and Pan, 1994). Thus the correlates of working models, as well as styles, may differ developmentally.

The pattern of findings is consistent with our hypotheses concerning the emergence of the different behavioral systems in romantic relationships. In middle adolescence, both romantic partners and friends are expected to be affiliative figures, and thus we expected correspondence between the representations of these relationships. In late adolescence, the links between representations of romantic relationships and relationships with parents may be more apparent as romantic relationships develop and as caregiving and attachment components begin to become more important. The links may also become stronger as relationships with parents become more egalitarian in nature.

The Nature of Change

Up to this point we have suggested that views may change with age or over the course of the development of a relationship. The data presented here are consistent with this idea, but further work needs to be done to determine precisely what may change or differ as a function of age or relationship status.

Most of the results presented here were concerned with overt relational styles and not internal working models of relationships. Some of the findings could simply reflect differences in the perceptions of their current behavior in romantic relationships rather than stable differences in their perceptions of how they approach issues of intimacy and closeness in romantic relationships. The links between romantic relationship status and one's romantic views could be accounted for by this explanation, as could other research that has found that some individuals with secure styles switch to an insecure style after a breakup, and some insecure avoidants become secure when they become involved in a new relationship (Kirkpatrick and Hazan, 1994).

At the same time, this explanation does not seem to provide a full account of these or other investigators' results. Even after controlling for relationship status differences, age differences were found for romantic style scores. The links among the style scores for different types of relationships also suggest that the romantic style scores are not just reflections of current romantic behavior. Additionally, styles are relatively stable over time, and in fact more stable than particular relationships (Kirkpatrick and Hazan, 1994). Finally, although the data are limited, the results obtained with the working model measures typically paralleled the results found on the style measures. Thus it appears that the results do not simply reflect the current status of an individual's romantic experiences, but further work is needed to determine the relative contributions of current experiences and stable predispositions. Further work is also needed to determine whether working models change over the course of development.

We also need to determine exactly what about these representations or these relationships seems to change. One possibility is that the differences reflect differences in the *frequency* with which romantic partners are tuned to fulfill these various functions. For example, as relationships develop, individuals may seek out their romantic partners more often as affiliative or attachment figures. Similar changes may occur as individuals grow older. The increase in the supportiveness of romantic relationships from high school to college found in the Furman and Buhrmester (1992) study is certainly consistent with this idea. Moreover, the age differences in the style scores for relationships with parents and friends also parallel differences in the perceptions of support found in the Furman and Buhrmester study. That is, women's perceptions of support from mother increase from high school to college and both genders' perceptions of support from father tend to increase. At the same time, perceptions of support from same-sex friends decrease from high school to college. The measures of style and support are, however, self-report measures, and it will be important to determine if such differences occur in the frequency of actual behavior.

The observed differences could also reflect differences in how *skillfully* individuals use romantic partners to fulfill different functions. For example, as they grow older, individuals may be more skillful in eliciting comfort from their partners when they are feeling upset. Similarly, individuals may also become more skillful over the course of particular relationships as they learn about their partners. This idea is supported by other findings with our college sample. Participants completed an adaptation of Buhrmester's (1990) Adolescent Interpersonal Competence Questionnaire, which assessed perceived skillfulness in romantic relationships. Women in exclusive relationships tended to have higher ratings of skillfulness than those who were casually dating, m's = 3.71 versus 3.47, $t(51) = 1.99$, $p < .06$. Ratings of skillfulness were also positively correlated with secure romantic style scores, $r = .56$, $p < .01$, and negatively correlated with preoccupied and dismissing scores, r's = $-.44$ and $-.31$, respectively, p's < .05.

Finally, changes could occur in appraisals of *felt security*. For example, over the course of a relationship that has been relatively supportive in nature, individuals may feel increasingly certain of the other person's availability and responsiveness. Theoretically, one would expect that frequency, skillfulness, and felt security would covary. Even if they do covary, however, the age differences or relationship status differences may not occur on all three variables. For example, it seems quite possible that late adolescents may turn to their romantic partners more often and more skillfully, but middle adolescents may feel just as secure (or insecure) as late adolescents. Alternatively, each could affect the other, leading to changes in all three variables.

An Agenda for the Future

Until quite recently, adolescent romantic relationships had received little attention from social scientists. The studies that are now emerging illustrate that these relationships are not the same as adult relationships, but they are of scientific interest, both as potential precursors to subsequent relationships and as interesting phenomena in their own right. The findings reported in this chapter provide evidence of the developmental nature of these relationships. At the same time, we have only scratched the surface of these relationships and the changes they undergo. As pointed out in the preceding section, it is unclear exactly what seems to change with age or relational experience. Several other issues also warrant further attention.

First, the present conceptualization has emphasized how romantic partners may serve as important figures in the attachment, caregiving, affiliative, and sexual systems. As yet, however, we know relatively little about how these functions are fulfilled in these relationships. For that matter, we know little about these processes in adulthood either, as relatively few observational studies have been conducted on dating and romantic relationships. Such work seems to be an essential foundation for understanding the nature of adolescent romantic relationships and the roles they play in psychosocial development.

Research is also needed on the emergence of these relationships in early adolescents' social networks. The initial relationships are short and ungainly in nature, but we need to examine their potential influence on romantic self-concept and peer status. The role of relationships with parents and same-and other-sex peers in the emergence of these relationships also warrants investigation. The studies presented here and in other research (Furman, in press; Connolly, Furman, and Konarski, 1997; Connolly and Johnson, 1996) demonstrate links in middle and late adolescence, but studies on the ties in early adolescence have not yet been conducted.

Another important topic to examine is the transformation these relationships undergo over the course of adolescence. When do individuals began to turn to partners as attachment, sexual, and affiliation figures? When do they began to provide care or support? What characteristics of individuals, partners, and relationships are associated with seeking out or fulfilling these different functions? How do they become integrated?

The studies presented here demonstrate differences as a function of age and of relationship status, but the research was cross-sectional in nature. We have inferred that the observed *differences* reflect *developmental changes* over the course of age or relationship development, but longitudinal work is needed to rule out alternative explanations, such as cohort or selection effects. Longitudinal studies of relationship development could also help us understand the transformations in affiliative, attachment, caregiving, and sexual features.

Such research could also shed light on the impact of both present relationships and past relationships. In this study we found that romantic views are related to the current status of the relationship, but we do not know whether such views have a long-term impact on relationship experiences or subsequent relationships. Longitudinal work is also needed to determine the causal links among parent-adolescent, peer, and romantic relationships.

Finally, the present chapter has focused on *common* changes that occur over the course of particular relationships or with age and experience. As noted in the beginning of the chapter, we do not expect that all individuals would follow these developmental patterns, nor do we mean to imply that the common paths are inherently better than various alternatives. In our ongoing research on romantic relationships, we have been most struck by the diversity of these relationships and the adolescents' experiences in them. The descriptions of common changes are an important initial step in understanding social processes and development, but ultimately we will need to examine the developmental changes of particular individuals and changes over the course of particular relationships. Longitudinal studies of individual trajectories or growth curves will be needed to understand the different courses and their causes and consequences. Such work should lead to a better understanding of these richly developmental phenomena.

References

Bartholomew, K., and Shaver, P. R. "Methods of Assessing Adult Attachment: Do They Converge?" In T. A. Simpson and W. S. Rhodes (eds.), *Attachment Theory and Close Relationships.* New York: Guilford Press, in press.

Borman-Spurrell, E., Allen, J. P., Hauser, S. T., Carter, A., and Coie-Detke, H. "Assessing Adult Attachment: A Comparison of Interview-Based and Self-Report Methods." Unpublished manuscript, 1993.

Bowlby, J. *Attachment and Loss,* Vol. 2: *Separation.* New York: Basic Books, 1973.

Brown, B. B. "You're Going with Whom?! Peer Group Influences on Adolescent Romantic Relationships." In W. Furman, B. B. Brown, and C. Feiring (eds.), *Contemporary Perspectives on Adolescent Romantic Relationships.* New York: Cambridge University Press, in press.

Brown, B. B., Eicher, S. A., and Petrie, S. "The Importance of Peer Group ('Crowd') Affiliation in Adolescence." *Journal of Adolescence,* 1986, *9,* 73–96.

Buhrmester, D. "Intimacy of Friendship, Interpersonal Competence, and Adjustment During Preadolescence and Adolescence." *Child Development,* 1990, *61,* 1101–1111.

Connell, J. C., and Furman, W. "Conceptual and Methodological Issues in the Study of Transitions." In R. Harmon and R. Emde (eds.), *Continuity and Discontinuity in Development.* New York: Plenum, 1984.

Connolly, J., Furman, W., and Konarski, R. "The Role of Peers in the Emergence of Romantic Relationships in Adolescence." Unpublished manuscript, 1997.

Connolly, J. A., and Johnson, A. M. "Adolescents' Romantic Relationships and the Structure and Quality of Their Close Interpersonal Ties." *Personal Relationships,* 1996, *3,* 185–195.

Crowell, J. A., Holtzworth-Munroe, A. H., Treboux, D., Waters, E., Stuart, G. L., and Hutchinson, G. "Assessing Working Models: A Comparison of the Adult Attachment Interview with Self-Report Measures of Attachment Relationships." Unpublished manuscript, 1993.

Diamond, L. M., Savin-Williams, R. C., and Dube, E. M. "Sex, Dating, Passionate Friendships, and Romance: Intimate Peer Relations Among Lesbian, Gay, and Bisexual Adolescents." In W. Furman, B. B. Brown, and C. Feiring (eds.), *Contemporary Perspectives on Adolescent Romantic Relationships.* New York: Cambridge University Press, in press.

Dion, K. K., and Dion, K. L. "Cultural Perspectives on Romantic Love." *Personal Relationships,* 1996, *3,* 5–19.

Dunphy, D. C. "The Social Structure of Urban Adolescent Peer Groups." *Sociometry,* 1963, *26,* 230–246.

Feiring, C. "Developing Concepts of Romance from Fifteen to Eighteen Years." Paper presented at the biennial meeting of the Society for Research in Child Development, New Orleans, March 1993.

Feiring, C. "Concepts of Romance in Fifteen-Year-Old Adolescents." *Journal of Research in Adolescence,* 1996, *6,* 181–200.

Furman, W. "The Role of Peer Relationships in Adolescent Romantic Relationships." In W. A. Collins and B. Laursen (eds.), *Minnesota Symposium on Child Development,* Vol 29: *Relationships as Developmental Contexts.* Hillsdale, N.J.: Erlbaum, in press.

Furman, W., and Buhrmester, D. "Age and Sex in Perceptions of Networks of Personal Relationships." *Child Development,* 1992, *63,* 103–115.

Furman, W., and Flanagan, A. "The Influence of Earlier Relationships on Marriage: An Attachment Perspective." In W. K. Halford and H. J. Markman (eds.), *Clinical Handbook of Marriage and Couples Interventions.* New York: Wiley, 1997.

Furman, W., and Simon, V. "Cognitive Representations of Adolescent Romantic Relationships." In W. Furman, B. B. Brown, and C. Feiring (eds.), *Contemporary Perspectives on Adolescent Romantic Relationships.* New York: Cambridge University Press, in press.

Furman, W., and Wehner, E. A. "Adolescent Romantic Relationships: A Developmental Perspective." Paper presented at biennial meeting of the Society for Research in Child Development, New Orleans, March 1993.

Furman, W., and Wehner, E. A. "Romantic Views: Toward a Theory of Adolescent Romantic Relationships." In R. Montemayor, G. R. Adams, and G. P. Gullota (eds.), *Advances in Adolescent Development,* Vol. 6: *Relationships During Adolescence.* Thousand Oaks, Calif.: Sage, 1994.

Gavin, L., and Furman, W. "Age Difference in Adolescents' Perceptions of Their Peer Groups." *Developmental Psychology,* 1989, *25,* 827–834.

Hazan, C., and Shaver, P. "Romantic Love Conceptualized as an Attachment Process." *Journal of Personality and Social Psychology,* 1987, *52,* 511–524.

Hazan, C., and Zeifman, D. "Sex and the Psychological Tether." In K. Bartholomew and D. Perlman (eds.), *Advances in Personal Relationships,* Vol. 5: *Attachment Processes in Adulthood.* London: Jessica Kingsley, 1994.

Kirkpatrick, L. A., and Hazan, C. "Attachment Styles and Close Relationships: A Four-Year Prospective Study." *Journal of Personality and Social Psychology,* 1994, *66,* 502–512.

Kobak, R. R. "The Attachment Interview Q-Set: Revised." Unpublished manuscript, University of Delaware, Newark, 1993.

Maccoby, E. E. "Gender as a Social Category." *Developmental Psychology,* 1988, *24,* 755–765.

Maccoby, E. E. "Gender and Relationships: A Developmental Account." *American Psychologist,* 1990, *45,* 513–520.

Main, M., Kaplan, N., and Cassidy, J. "Security in Infancy, Childhood, and Adulthood: A Move to the Level of Representation." In I. Bretherton and E. Waters (eds.), *Growing Points of Attachment Theory and Research.* Monograph for the Society for Research in Child Development. Chicago: University of Chicago Press, 1985.

Shaver, P., Furman, W., and Buhrmester, D. "Aspects of a Life Transition: Network Changes, Social Skills and Loneliness." In S. Duck and D. Perlman (eds.), *The Sage Series in Personal Relationships,* Vol. 1. London: Sage, 1985.

Thornton, A. "The Courtship Process and Adolescent Sexuality." *Journal of Family Issues,* 1990, *11,* 239–273.

Treboux, D., Crowell, J. A., Owens, G., and Pan, H. S. "Attachment Behaviors and Working Models: Relations to Best Friendships and Romantic Relationships." Unpublished
manuscript, State University of New York at Stony Brook, 1994.
Wehner, E. A. "Adolescent Romantic Relationships: Attachment, Caregiving, Affiliation, and
Sex." Unpublished doctoral dissertation, University of Denver, 1992.

WYNDOL FURMAN is professor in the Department of Psychology, University of Denver.

ELIZABETH A. WEHNER is an instructor in the Department of Psychiatry, University
of Colorado Health Sciences Center.

Based on a comprehensive understanding of intimacy, and emerging from a systems theory, this chapter examines adolescent intimacy in close friendships and romantic relationships. Males and females deal differently with the balancing of closeness and individuality in the two types of close friendships. In addition, development of an intimate romantic relationship requires greater commitment for males than for females.

Intimate Relationships Among Adolescent Romantic Partners and Same-Sex Friends: Individual and Systemic Perspectives

Shmuel Shulman, Rachel Levy-Shiff, Peri Kedem, Eitan Alon

Throughout adolescence, close friendships are increasingly organized around intimacy (Jones and Dembo, 1989). Research on adolescent friendship and intimacy has converged on two central themes: closeness and individuality. *Closeness* refers to mutual empathy, love, and security (Sullivan, 1953). With age adolescents become aware that in a close relationship the needs of both participants must be addressed. Through rewarding exchanges, friends strongly influence the thoughts, feelings, and behavior of one another (Laursen, 1993). This closeness provides the impetus for self-disclosure, prompting discussion of personal matters such as sexuality, family problems, and money. Closeness thus captures the interpersonal processes whereby friends share important feelings and information (Reis and Shaver, 1988).

Individuality refers to the development of separate and distinct identities. According to Erikson (1963), establishing an identity requires the capacity to commit to a close relationship, allowing "fusion without fear of ego loss" (p. 264). Individuation emerges gradually during adolescence. Adolescents express personal styles and create unique selves, which are then shared in their close relationships. Thus the growing need for commitment and exclusivity should not be disconnected from the emergent impetus for individuation and responsibility for one's own actions (Blos, 1967).

The purpose of this chapter is to explore the nature of intimacy in adolescent romantic relationships. This will be done by presenting a comprehensive understanding of adolescent intimacy, and by comparing male and female expressions of intimacy in same-sex and romantic close relationships. In addition, emerging from a systemic perspective, we will explore differences in types of adolescent romantic relationship and their interdependence with same-sex close friendships.

Evidence to date suggests that there are sex differences in friendship intimacy. Adolescent female friends are reportedly closer and more inclined to self-disclosure than males (Camarena, Sarigiani, and Petersen, 1990; Jones and Dembo, 1989; Sharabany, Gershoni, and Hofman, 1981; Shulman, Laursen, Kalman, and Karpovsky, in press). A meta-analytic study also confirmed the trend toward less self-disclosure in boys' and men's friendships than in girls' and women's friendships (Dindia and Allen, 1992). Males tend to express themselves through separateness, characterizing friendship in terms of shared activities, whereas females perceive relatedness, emphasizing mutual closeness, and reciprocity in friendships (Smollar and Youniss, 1982).

These different intimacy patterns were found mostly in same-sex friendships. In contrast, within cross-gender friendships adolescent boys and young men both appeared willing to disclose to their female friends, and expected to become more disclosing in their adult spousal relationships (Reisman, 1990). Among married couples, no significant differences were found between husbands and wives on self-disclosure and expression of emotions (Merves-Okin, Amidon, and Berndt, 1991). Intimacy, measured in terms of caring, commitment, and communication, also showed no significant differences within couples (White and others, 1986). This suggests that within cross-gender and marital relationships, reciprocal self-disclosure between partners would be likely.

Furman, in his suggested theory on adolescent romantic relationships, also emphasizes the egalitarian nature of these relationships because they develop within the context of the peer group (Furman and Wehner, 1994). Within romantic relationships, one partner may serve as a caregiver for the other during a certain period of time, yet over time these roles are flexible and may change.

In a previous study, we designed a method to obtain a comprehensive view of a close relationship, particularly as it pertains to the balance of closeness and individuality (Shulman, Laursen, Kalman, and Karpovsky, in press). In our approach, intimacy is measured by the following dimensions:

Emotional closeness includes shared affect, availability, and instrumental assistance.

Control reflects one's tendency to control the other, or to insist on doing things one's own way.

Conformity assays similarity in appearance and ideas, as well as the importance of conforming on these issues.

Balanced relatedness indicates tolerance for differing opinions and ideas.

Respect for friend assesses mutual respect for individuation, competence, and uniqueness.

In addition, three dimensions of self-disclosure (*family, friends,* and *physical development*) are assessed.

This approach differs somewhat from descriptions that exclusively emphasize emotional closeness and self-disclosure (Reis and Shaver, 1988). It is also consistent with a systems theory perspective of close relationships, whereby the needs of the individual are negotiated alongside the needs of the relationship (Shulman, 1993). Results from the comprehensive understanding of intimacy reiterated sex differences on indices of self-disclosure and emotional closeness in same-sex close friendships. Regarding indices of individuality, girls described a greater tolerance toward differing opinions, whereas boys placed greater emphasis on similarity to their close friend as well as preference for unilateral decision making.

Building on the comprehensive understanding of intimacy, the first part of this study compares levels of intimacy, measured in terms of closeness and individuality, as reported by males and females in romantic and same-sex adolescent friendships.

A Systemic Approach to Adolescent Romantic Relationships

Few studies have examined individual differences in adolescent relationship intimacy. Research on adult romantic partners suggests that variations in intimacy produce three types of relationships: merger, pseudointimacy, and genuine intimacy (Orlofsky, 1976; Orlofsky, Marcia, and Lesser, 1973). *Merger relationships* lack balance and free expression. *Pseudointimate relationships* offer balanced roles and room to explore individuality, but little commitment to the relationship itself. *Genuine intimacy* is characterized by depth of roles, and by mutual commitment to the relationship. Weiss (1987) suggests that the maturity of a romantic relationship is reflected in the ability of partners to solve conflicts, in turn enhancing their sense of closeness.

In the study of same-sex friendship, research adapting a relationship typology from general systems theory (Minuchin, 1974; Reiss, 1981; Wynne, Rycoff, Day, and Hirsch, 1958; Wynne, 1970) has identified two types of adolescent friendships: interdependent and disengaged (Shulman, 1993). Comparison of interdependent and disengaged friendship pairs reveals consistent differences regarding their relational conceptions and behavior. Adolescents belonging to the interdependent type have a more solid view of friendship; they view it as an arena for joint activities and support. Conflicts are not perceived as a threat to the relationship. In this type of friendship, closeness does not preclude individuality. Disengaged friends, in contrast, lack an inherent sense of closeness. In the absence of closeness, the relationship is limited to providing companionship and assuaging loneliness. The fact that partners are not highly involved with each other protects them from conflict situations. Similar distinctions are hypothesized for adolescent romantic friendships.

Wynne (1986) emphasizes that intimacy is not only an experience but also an expression of an enduring relationship between partners. As such, it can be perceived as a system (Steinglass, 1978). The sense of intimacy experienced by one partner of the dyad cannot be disconnected from the nature and quality of intimacy experienced by the other. Studies of married couples show differential effects of husbands' and wives' characteristics on each other. For example, a husband's level of concern for his wife was positively related to the wife's maturity in several intimacy domains. A wife's level of concern for others, in contrast, was correlated with her husband's immaturity in major dimensions of intimacy (White and others, 1986). Together these contentions and findings suggest that the intimacy level of a romantic partner is related to both the mode of negotiation and the level of intimacy perceived by the other partner in the relationship.

As Furman and Wehner (1994) claim, romantic relationships in adolescence cannot be disconnected from peer relationships. In fact, they can be perceived as an integral part of the adolescent's social world. It is therefore reasonable to question the extent to which adolescent romantic relationships are also associated with the experience and perceptions adolescents have of their same-sex friendships. On the one hand, it might be argued, in line with Sullivan's (1953) theory and Furman and Wehner's (1994) conceptualization, that the sense of intimacy experienced with a close same-sex friend is transferred to, or serves as a model for, intimacy with a romantic partner. On the other hand, developmental approaches suggest that companionship and amount of time spent with same-sex friends decrease during adolescence, whereas with romantic partners these factors increase (Clark-Lempers, Lempers, and Ho, 1991; Larson and Richards, 1991). Thus the alternate assumption is that involvement with a same-sex friend may decrease the level of involvement with a romantic partner.

In sum, three questions are addressed in this study:

1. Do males and females report levels of intimacy in their romantic relationships similar to those found among married couples (White and others, 1986), or do they report different levels of intimacy, similar to data comparing males' and females' intimacy within same-sex close friendships (Camarena, Sarigiani, and Petersen, 1990; Jones and Dembo, 1989; Sharabany, Gershoni, and Hofman, 1981; Shulman, Laursen, Kalman, and Karpovsky, in press)?
2. Does intimacy vary across different types of adolescent romantic relationships, with partners belonging to the interdependent type reporting higher levels of closeness and respect for individuality compared to partners belonging to the disengaged type?
3. How do male and female partners affect each other's level of intimacy, and to what extent are experiences in same-sex friendships carried into romantic relationships?

Method

Subjects. Forty-three pairs of adolescent romantic couples (age range 17–19; mean age: females = 17.1, males = 17.4) were included in the study. Only couples who maintained a romantic relationship for at least three months were included in the study. All subjects were Israeli high school students residing in urban or suburban areas.

Instruments and Procedure. Two scales were used to assess intimacy and self-disclosure. Scale items were adapted from established instruments (originally designed for college students and young adults) that assess characteristics of friend, romantic, and marital relationships (Jourard, 1964; Schaefer and Edgerton, 1979; Sharabany, Gershoni, and Hofman, 1981). The comprehensive procedure of scale construction and the scale's psychometric properties are described in Shulman, Laursen, Kalman, and Karpovsky (in press).

The intimacy scale consists of the following five subscales; the first three reflect closeness, and the last two reflect individuality:

Emotional closeness: This subscale measures the degree to which friends perceive each other as close, available, and willing to help.
Control: This subscale measures the extent to which a partner shows a tendency to control the other, or to insist on doing things his or her own way.
Similarity: This subscale refers to the extent to which friends perceive themselves as similar in appearance or ideas, and the degree to which being similar is important to them.
Balanced relatedness: This subscale measures the degree to which differing opinions and ideas expressed by a partner are respected and negotiated within the relationship.
Respect for the friend: This subscale measures the extent to which a partner respects the other and perceives him or her to be competent.

Self-disclosure was assayed in three subject areas: *family, the friendship,* and *body,* measuring the extent to which a partner tends to disclose matters pertaining to his/her family, matters pertaining to the relationship with the partner, and matters pertaining to his or her body and physical development.

Subjects twice rated intimacy items on a four-point scale ranging from low (1) to high (4). The first rating was in reference to the romantic partner: "To what extent do the following statements characterize your relationship with your boyfriend/girlfriend?" The second referred to the same-sex close friend: "To what extent do the following statements characterize your relationship with your close friend?" The five intimacy subscales and the self-disclosure subscales each comprised eight items.

Romantic relationship types were identified with an adapted version of the Card Sort Problem Solving Procedure (Reiss, 1981), a technique with demonstrated efficacy in identifying different types of adolescent friendships (see Shulman, 1993). Pairs of friends were presented with separate sets of sixteen cards; each card contained a row of letters, varying in order and length. Subjects were instructed to use any criteria they liked to sort the cards into any number of piles. The task was divided into two phases. First, each adolescent sorted his or her own cards separately, without speaking. Second, each adolescent again sorted the cards separately, but this time communication was permitted. Instructions were not provided regarding dyadic agreement during the second phase, so both separate and joint sorting were possible.

Problem-solving behavior was coded on two dimensions: *configuration* and *coordination* (see Reiss, 1981). Configuration reflected changes from the first to the second card sorts; it denoted the extent to which friends influenced each other when given the opportunity to interact. Positive scores on configuration (greater than zero) indicated that interaction improved problem solving, while negative scores (less than zero) indicated that interaction hindered problem solving. Coordination reflected both solution similarity and difference (in standard deviations) in the time taken to complete the second sort. Small standard deviations indicated that participants finished trials at the same time. A median split defined coordination criteria. High coordination scores (sort similarity greater than .68 and sort standard deviations less than four seconds) indicated that friends worked together. Low coordination scores (sort similarity less than .68 and sort standard deviations greater than four seconds) indicated that friends resisted cooperation.

In addition, interaction between partners during the joint problem-solving task was recorded and later rated by two judges on a 1 to 5 rating scale for competition, cooperation, and control.

Two romantic relationship types were identified: *interdependent* and *disengaged*. A total of twenty-six couples qualified as interdependent. These dyads were high on coordination (M sort similarity = .91, SD = .13, and M sort SD = 2.44 seconds, SD = 1.37), high on configuration (M = .09, SD = .13) and low on competition (3 and below). A total of seventeen couples qualified as disengaged. These dyads were low on coordination (M sort similarity = .51, SD = .21, and M sort SD = 6.64 seconds, SD = 4.91), low on configuration (M = −.07, SD = .10), and high on competition (higher than 4).

Results

Intimacy Within Romantic Relationships and Close Friendships. Separate sets of analyses were conducted on the intimacy and self-disclosure scales.

Intimacy. A MANOVA was conducted with four levels of repeated measures (female report on romantic relationship and on same-sex close friendship, and male report on romantic relationship and on same-sex close friendship) and five intimacy subscales. Intimacy was the dependent variable. A significant main effect emerged for the four levels of male/female repeated measures, Wilks (3, 40) = 13.23, $p < .0001$. Follow-up ANOVAs on each intimacy subscale revealed significant differences across the four repeated measures on emotional closeness, similarity, control, and respect for friend. F values, means, and standard deviations are presented in Table 3.1. Scheffe follow-up contrasts elaborated the repeated measures differences. As can be seen, males reported lower levels of emotional closeness, similarity, and control only when describing their same-sex friendships. They reported a similar level of intimacy in their romantic relationships, as did their female partners. Females reported similar levels on intimacy indices in their romantic and same-sex close relationships. Females reported a higher level of respect for friend than did males in both types of close relationships.

Self-Disclosure. A MANOVA was conducted with four levels of repeated measures (female report on romantic relationship and on same-sex close relationship, and male report on romantic relationship and on same-sex close relationship) and three self-disclosure subscales. Self-disclosure was the dependent variable. A significant main effect emerged for the four levels of male/female repeated measures Wilks $(3, 40) = 22.48$, $p < .001$. Follow-up ANOVAs on each self-disclosure subscale revealed significant differences across the four repeated measures on the three subscales: friendship, family, and physical development F values, means, and standard deviations are presented in

Table 3.1. Intimacy and Self-Disclosure Levels for Males and Females in Romantic and Same-Sex Friendships: Means, Standard Deviations, and Wilks Values

	FM	MF	FF	MM	
Emotional closeness	3.36[a]	3.29[a]	3.16[b]	2.97[c]	Wilks $(3,40) = 8.39$***
	(0.34)	(0.47)	(0.41)	(0.40)	
Similarity	2.47[a]	2.32[a]	2.37[a]	2.19[b]	Wilks $(3,40) = 3.51$*
	(0.49)	(0.53)	(0.36)	(0.63)	
Control	1.51[a]	1.64[b]	1.61[a,b]	1.39[c]	Wilks $(3,40) = 10.79$***
	(0.31)	(0.37)	(0.34)	(0.27)	
Balanced relatedness	3.07	2.96	3.03	3.05	Wilks $(3,40) = 0.74$
	(0.38)	(0.34)	(0.37)	(0.32)	
Respect for a friend	3.11[a]	2.87[b]	3.19[a]	2.85[b]	Wilks $(3,40) = 15.82$***
	(0.38)	(0.31)	(0.40)	(0.38)	
Self-disclosure/ friendship	2.79[a]	3.22[b]	2.88[a]	2.40[c]	Wilks $(3,40) = 20.33$**
	(0.64)	(0.48)	(0.60)	(0.39)	
Self-disclosure/ family	3.03[a]	3.11[a]	2.93[a]	2.52[b]	Wilks $(3,40) = 4.76$**
	(0.75)	(0.68)	(0.88)	(0.81)	
Self-disclosure/ physical development	2.77[a]	3.22[b]	3.44[b]	2.53[c]	Wilks $(3,40) = 26.63$**
	(0.86)	(0.55)	(0.51)	(0.55)	

Note: Within rows, means with different superscripts indicate significant differences in Scheffe follow-up contrasts ($p < .05$). FM = female report on male romantic partner; MF = male report on female romantic partner; FF = female report on female friendship; MM = male report on male friendship.

*$p < .05$.
**$p < .01$.
***$p < .001$.

Table 3.1. Scheffe follow-up contrasts elaborated the repeated measures differences. As can be seen, males reported lower levels of self-disclosure in their same-sex friendships only. Within their romantic relationships, males reported higher levels of self-disclosure than did their female partners, in the indices of friendship and physical development. Females revealed a similar level on the friendship and family self-disclosure indices in their romantic and same-sex friendships, yet they showed a low tendency toward disclosure to their boyfriends in reference to their body and physical development. Disclosure on this domain was more often expressed to their same-sex close friends than to their romantic partners.

Intimacy Among Interdependent and Disengaged Relationship Types. Next we compare the interdependent and disengaged couples.

Intimacy. A MANOVA was conducted with 2 (friendship types) $\times$ 2 (sex) levels of between-subject independent variables. The intimacy subscales (measuring intimacy in the romantic relationship) were the dependent variable. Results yielded main effects for friendship type Wilks $(4, 38) = 2.94, p < .05$; and for sex Wilks $(4, 38), = 8.41, p < .001$. They also yielded a significant interaction of friendship type $\times$ sex Wilks $(4, 38), = 4.24, p < .001$. Interdependent romantic partners reported a higher level of emotional closeness (M = 3.43, SD = 0.32) in comparison to disengaged romantic partners (M = 3.16, SD = 0.41). Interdependent partners also reported lower levels of control (M = 1.48, SD = 0.32) than did their disengaged counterparts (M = 1.72, SD = 0.32). Significant interactions revealed the sex differences to exist only within the disengaged groups. Males and females in the interdependent group reported similar levels of intimacy on all five of the indices; in the disengaged group, males reported less similarity and less respect for friend than did females. Means, standard deviations, and F values are presented in Table 3.2.

Self-Disclosure. A MANOVA was conducted with 2 (friendship types) $\times$ 2 (sex) levels of between-subject independent variables. The self-disclosure subscales were the dependent variable. Results yielded a significant main effect for sex Wilks $(2,40), = 5.49, p < .001$; and a significant interaction of friendship type $\times$ sex Wilks $(2,40), = 5.73, p < .001$. Males tended to disclose more to their girlfriends than females did to their boyfriends, on issues pertaining to the romantic relationship, M = 2.79 and M = 3.22, respectively. Follow-up of the interactions revealed that males in the disengaged type tended to disclose more on family issues than did males in the interdependent type. Females in the interdependent type tended to disclose less than did females in the disengaged type, on issues pertaining to physical development. Means, standard deviations, and F values are presented in Table 3.2.

Intimacy in Romantic Relationships: A Systems Perspective

Hierarchical regressions were conducted to determine which variables moderate a partner's level for each of the intimacy and self-disclosure indices. Regressions were computed for females and males separately. The order of inclusion of the variables was as follows:

Table 3.2. Intimacy and Self-Disclosure Levels for Males and Females in Interdependent and Disengaged Romantic Relationships: Means, Standard Deviations, and F Values

	Interdependent (N = 26)		Disengaged (N = 17)		F Type	F Sex	F Interaction
	FM	MF	FM	MF			
Emotional closeness	3.41	3.45	3.28	3.05	7.32*	1.52	3.23
	(0.34)	(0.31)	(0.32)	(0.57)			
Similarity	2.41	2.46	2.55	2.11	0.62	4.55*	7.36*
	(0.58)	(0.57)	(0.32)	(0.41)			
Control	1.41	1.56	1.68	1.76	10.58*	2.66	0.26
	(0.33)	(0.29)	(0.20)	(0.45)			
Balanced relatedness	3.16	3.00	2.92	2.91	3.73	1.61	1.12
	(0.36)	(0.25)	(0.36)	(0.46)			
Respect for a friend	3.06	2.99	3.20	2.69	0.75	29.57*	16.82*
	(0.46)	(0.28)	(0.18)	(0.27)			
Self-disclosure/ friendship	2.78	3.10	2.80	3.40	1.11	22.20	*2.14
	(0.53)	(0.52)	(0.80)	(0.31)			
Self-disclosure/ family	3.02	2.98	3.04	3.31	0.68	2.20	4.18*
	(0.70)	(0.75)	(0.84)	(0.51)			
Self-disclosure/ physical develop- ment	2.59	3.18	3.04	3.19	2.63	4.71*	1.60
	(0.91)	(0.59)	(0.71)	(0.48)			

Note: FM = female report on male romantic partner; MF = male report on female romantic partner.

$*p < .05$

1. The length of time, in months, that partners consider themselves a romantic couple
2. The partner's level on the specific index
3. The type of romantic relationship
4. The subject's level on the specific index in his or her same-sex friendship

Results of the hierarchical regressions for females and males are presented in Table 3.3. As can be seen, males' levels on intimacy measures were far better explained than those of females. Females' and males' levels of intimacy were moderated by that of their partner, and by the type of relationship in which they were involved, yet males were more affected by the quality of the relationship. Females' intimacy was also affected by the duration of the relationship in which they were involved. Males' same-sex friendships were an important moderator of the intimacy experienced in their romantic relationships. Thus, the more emotionally close males were to their same sex friend, the more they tolerated his differing views and respected him, the less close they were to their girlfriend and the less they respected her individuality. Conversely, both a sense of similarity to their same sex friend for males and a tendency to control their friend for females served as a model for the

Table 3.3. Predictors of Males' and Females' Levels of Intimacy: Hierarchical Regressions, Beta Values, and Significance

Emotional closeness

Females	R^2	Beta	Males	R^2	Beta
Step 1: Time	.00	−.04	Step 1: Time	.02	−.14
Step 2: Boyfriend's EC	.10	.31	Step 2: Girlfriend's EC	.12	.31*
Step 3: Relational type	.10	.08	Step 3: Relational type	.20	.30*
Step 4: EC in same sex	.11	.00	Step 4: EC in same sex	.65	−.70***

Similarity

Females	R^2	Beta	Males	R^2	Beta
Step 1: Time	.12	.35*	Step 1: Time	.10	.32*
Step 2: Boyfriend's SM	.15	.17	Step 2: Girlfriend's SM	.13	.18
Step 3: Relational type	.18	.21	Step 3: Relational type	.34	.45**
Step 4: SM in same sex	.18	.05	Step 4: SM in same sex	.46	.38***

Control

Females	R^2	Beta	Males	R^2	Beta
Step 1: Time	.13	.35*	Step 1: Time	.00	−.05
Step 2: Boyfriend's CT	.15	.15	Step 2: Girlfriend's CT	.03	.17
Step 3: Relational type	.21	−.25*	Step 3: Relational type	.03	.07
Step 4: CT in same sex	.31	.34**	Step 4: CT in same sex	.08	.22

Balanced relatedness

Females	R^2	Beta	Males	R^2	Beta
Step 1: Time	.16	−.40*	Step 1: Time	.01	−.12
Step 2: Boyfriend's BR	.20	.19	Step 2: Girlfriend's BR	.06	.22
Step 3: Relational type	.23	−.17	Step 3: Relational type	.06	.05
Step 4: BR in same sex	.26	−.24	Step 4: BR in same sex	.47	−.68***

Respect for a friend

Females	R^2	Beta	Males	R^2	Beta
Step 1: Time	.05	.23	Step 1: Time	.00	.09
Step 2: Boyfriend's RFr	.16	.32*	Step 2: Girlfriend's RFr	.12	.37
Step 3: Relational type	.23	−.30*	Step 3: Relational type	.28	.41**
Step 4: RFr in same sex	.27	−.18	Step 4: RFr in same sex	.39	−.34***

*$P < .05$
**$P < .01$
***$P < .001$

romantic relationship, respectively. Additional hierarchical regressions showed that both females' and males' self-disclosure was moderated by that of their romantic partner and by the quality of the relationship.

Discussion

These findings appear to shed new light on our understanding of sex differences in adolescent intimacy, and also to tell us how adolescent males and females deal with issues of closeness and individuality in their intimate relationships. In the present study, in comparison to adolescent females, adolescent males reported lower levels of intimacy in their same-sex friendships, yet within their romantic relationships they reported similar levels of intimacy. These results demonstrate that adolescent males' perception of intimacy in their romantic relationships resembles that of married males (Merves-Okin, Amidon, and Berndt, 1991; White and others, 1986).

These results suggest that sex differences on intimacy may be a result of preference rather than ability. In their relationships with fellow males, males are probably more threatened by anything that could compromise their individuality (Gilligan, 1982), whereas in relationships with romantic partners, competition is less an issue and therefore males may allow themselves to be more intimate, thereby disclosing more to their romantic partners. Moreover, as Gilligan claims, as boys mature they must learn to connect, and they do so with their romantic partner.

In our study, however, when intimacy was measured in terms of closeness and individuality, the higher levels of intimacy for males in romantic relationships were found only on indices of closeness and self-disclosure, but not on indices reflecting individuality. For example, males reported a lower level of respect for friend in both types of close relationships than did females. It is probable that the males' need for closeness with their romantic partner does not suppress their need to assert individuality. As has been found in other studies, men are more likely than women to interrupt their partners (Leaper and Anderson, this volume). Due to fear of loss of individuality, husbands tend more to withdraw during conflict with their spouses (Bergman, 1995). Females who experience themselves primarily as part of relationships (Gilligan, 1982) are at ease to be close with both their female friends and their romantic partners. Overall, women's balance of closeness and individuality in their close relationships is different than that of their male partners, though they may certainly feel close to each other.

Theory and research have consistently emphasized the need to study qualitative differences in relationship functioning. For instance, major advances in our understanding of parent-child relationships emerged after attachment theorists applied qualitative categories to behavioral responses in a laboratory task. Our results point to differential dynamics governing the relationship in interdependent and disengaged types. Interdependent partners displayed a relationship that emphasized more emotional closeness and less exerted control. Disengaged partners reported a lower level of emotional closeness and a higher level of control. In the interdependent type, friends are attracted to each other by their sense of closeness and respect. In the disengaged type, in contrast, where closeness is less expressed and experienced, partners must employ control to keep the relationship from falling apart.

Together these findings recall our previous study of the typology of same-sex friendships in adolescence (Shulman, 1993; Shulman, Laursen, Kalman, and Karpovsky, in press). Moreover, the results reiterate what systems theorists have described as a requirement, namely, the importance of balancing closeness and separateness in order to balance the needs of family members, and the fact that systems create different balances to keep members together (Minuchin, 1974; Steinglass, 1978). Steinglass (1978) contended that maintaining a relationship by controlling the other requires a higher level of energy and may hinder an individual's sense that his or her needs are truly respected. In our study, it was the male partner who was adversely affected by the disengaged type of relationship.

It is interesting that males were especially sensitive to the quality of their romantic relationships. Males in the disengaged type reported lower levels of intimacy than did males in the interdependent type, whereas females in both relationship types reported similar levels of intimacy. It is probable, as suggested by previous studies, that females who throughout their development are expected to stay connected in meaningful ways (Papp, 1989) are more capable than males of expressing higher levels of intimacy in various types of close relationships. Males are less at ease in expressing their intimate feelings, and they do so only once they feel comfortable and truly accepted in a relationship. In the disengaged type, males felt less similar to their partner and less respected by her, and also showed a tendency to report a low sense of emotional closeness to their girlfriend.

Results of the self-disclosure levels in the two friendship types are counterintuitive; males belonging to the disengaged type disclosed more on issues pertaining to their families, while females belonging to the disengaged type disclosed more on issues pertaining to their body and physical development. We speculate that people possibly feel more at ease to disclose to strangers in some circumstances (Wolff, 1950). It is possible that disclosure to someone who is not too close, such as a partner in the disengaged type, is perceived as more secure. In addition, higher levels of disclosure were not related to more reciprocity between partners. On the contrary, self-disclosure among disengaged partners on issues pertaining to physical development was asymmetrical.

In general, results showed that the sense of intimacy among romantic partners is affected by the nature of the relationship with the other. In this sense, results for adolescent romantic partners show similarity to marital partners where the relationship experience of one partner affects the other (Collins and Reed, 1990). Males, however, are more affected by their partners than are females. For males, a romantic relationship is probably a different domain than a friendship, and requires greater commitment. Being involved in a same-sex friendship was related to a lower level of intimacy in their romantic relationship. As discussed earlier, males must learn to connect. For the adolescent male, intimacy with a romantic partner is a new and different experience. As such, the relationship can develop once the adolescent male is committed to it, and when the female partner invests in the relationship.

This additional distinction between males and females raises a theoretical question. In their theory, Furman and Wehner (1994) claim that in friendships children develop the ability to be intimate in a reciprocal and mutual fashion. Results of our study can hardly lay support to this claim. Only in two instances did experience in same-sex friendships explain intimacy with the romantic partner. First, the more males felt similar to their same-sex close friend, the more they felt similar to their girlfriend. Second, among females, the experience of controlling their friend explained the level of control in their romantic relationship. However, on three indices of intimacy—emotional closeness, balanced relatedness, and respect for friend—as well as on self-disclosure regarding the friendship, being more involved in same-sex friendships among males was related to a lower level of involvement with their romantic partner. We speculate that at a certain point in their development males are supposed to become less involved with their male peers and to invest in their romantic relationship. This is less required of females, probably suggesting different sequences for males and females in the development of dating.

In closing, we note that our findings lead us to suggest that the distinction between adolescent males and females with regard to friendships and romantic relationships is more complex than we had anticipated. The two genders cope differently with the balancing of closeness and individuality in their close friendships. In addition, experience in a close friendship carries with it a different influence on romantic relationships for females than for males. Future studies could further tell us how males and females shift from close friendships to romantic relationships during adolescence.

References

Bergman, S. G. "Men's Psychological Development: A Relational Perspective." In R. F. Levant and W. S. Pollack (eds.), *A New Psychology of Men*. New York: Basic Books, 1995.

Blos, P. "The Second Individuation Process of Adolescence." *The Psychoanalytic Study of the Child*, 1967, *22*, 162–186.

Camarena, P. M., Sarigiani, P. A., and Petersen, A. C. "Gender-Specific Pathways to Intimacy in Early Adolescence." *Journal of Youth and Adolescence*, 1990, *19*, 19–32.

Clark-Lempers, D. S., Lempers, J. D., and Ho, C. "Early, Middle, and Late Adolescents' Perceptions of Their Relationships with Significant Others." *Journal of Adolescent Research*, 1991, *6*, 296–315.

Collins, N. L., and Reed, S. J. "Adult Attachment, Working Models and Relationship Quality in Dating Couples." *Journal of Personality and Social Psychology*, 1990, *58*, 644–663.

Dindia, K., and Allen, M. "Sex Differences in Self-Disclosure: A Meta-Analysis." *Psychological Bulletin*, 1992, *112*, 106–124.

Erikson, E. H. *Childhood and Society*. New York: Norton, 1963.

Furman, W., and Wehner, E. A. "Romantic Views: Toward a Theory of Adolescent Romantic Relationships." In R. Montemayor (ed.), *Advances in Adolescent Development*, Vol. 3: *Relationships in Adolescence*. Thousand Oaks, Calif.: Sage, 1994.

Gilligan, C. *In a Different Voice: Psychological Theory and Women's Development*. Cambridge, Mass.: Harvard University Press, 1982.

Jones, P. J., and Dembo, M. H. "Age and Sex Role Differences in Intimate Friendships During Childhood and Adolescence." *Merrill-Palmer Quarterly*, 1989, *35*, 445–462.

Jourard, S. *The Transparent Self*. New York: Van Nostrand Reinhold, 1964.

Larson, R., and Richards, M. H. "Daily Companionship in Late Childhood and Early Adolescence." *Child Development*, 1991, *62*, 284–300.

Laursen, B. *Adolescent Friendships*. San Francisco: Jossey-Bass, 1993.

Merves-Okin, L., Amidon, E., and Berndt, F. "Perceptions of Intimacy in Marriage: A Study of Married Couples." *American Journal of Family Therapy*, 1991, *19*, 110–118.

Minuchin, S. *Families and Family Therapy*. Cambridge, Mass.: Harvard University Press, 1974.

Orlofsky, J. L. "Intimacy Status: Relationship to Interpersonal Perception." *Journal of Youth and Adolescence*, 1976, 5, 73–88.

Orlofsky, J. L., Marcia, J. E., and Lesser, I. "Ego Identity Status and the Intimacy Versus Isolation Crisis of Young Adulthood." *Journal of Personality and Social Psychology*, 1973, 7, 211–219.

Papp, P. "The Godfather." In M. Walters, B. Carter, P. Papp, and O. Silverstein (eds.), *The Invisible Web: Gender Pattern in Family Relationships*. New York: Guilford Press, 1989.

Reis, H. T., and Shaver, P. "Intimacy as an Interpersonal Process." In S. Duck (ed.), *Handbook of Personal Relationships: Theory, Relationships, and Intervention*. New York: Wiley, 1988.

Reisman, J. M. "Intimacy in Same-Sex Friendships." *Sex Roles*, 1990, 23, 65–82.

Reiss, D. *The Family's Construction of Reality*. Cambridge, Mass.: Harvard University Press, 1981.

Schaefer, E. S., and Edgerton, M. *Marital Autonomy and Relatedness Inventory*. Chapel Hill: University of North Carolina, 1979.

Sharabany, R., Gershoni, R., and Hofman, J. E. "Girlfriend, Boyfriend: Age and Sex Differences in Intimate Friendship." *Developmental Psychology*, 1981, 17, 800–808.

Shulman, S. "Early and Middle Adolescent Close Friendships: Typology and Friendship Reasoning." In B. Laursen (ed.), *Adolescent Friendships*. San Francisco: Jossey-Bass, 1993.

Shulman, S., Laursen, B., Kalman, Z., and Karpovsky, S. "Adolescent Intimacy: Revisited." *Journal of Youth and Adolescence*, in press.

Smollar, J., and Youniss, J. "Social Development Through Friendship." In K. H. Rubin and H. S. Ross (eds.), *Peer Relationships and Social Skills in Childhood*. New York: Springer-Verlag, 1982.

Steinglass, P. "The Conceptualization of Marriage from a Systems Theory Perspective." In T. J. Paulino and B. S. McGradey (eds.), *Marriage and Marital Therapy*. New York: Brunner/Mazel, 1978.

Sullivan, H. S. *The Interpersonal Theory of Psychiatry*. New York: Norton, 1953.

Weiss, A. G. "Privacy and Intimacy: Apart and a Part." *Journal of Humanistic Psychology*, 1987, 27, 118–125.

White, K. M., Speiseman, J. C., Jackson, D., Bartis, S., and Costos, D. "Intimacy Maturity and Its Correlates in Young Married Couples." *Journal of Personality and Social Psychology*, 1986, 50, 152–162.

Wolff, K. H. *The Sociology of George Simmel* (chap. 3, "The Stranger"). New York: Free Press, 1950.

Wynne, C. L. "Communication Disorders and the Quest for Relatedness in Families of Schizophrenics." *American Journal of Psychoanalysis*, 1970, 30, 100–114.

Wynne, C. L. "The Quest for Intimacy." *Journal of Marital and Family Therapy*, 1986, 12, 383–394.

Wynne, C. L., Rycoff, I., Day, J., and Hirsch, S. "Pseudomutuality in Families of Schizophrenics." *Psychiatry*, 1958, 1, 205–250.

Youniss, J., and Smollar, J. *Adolescents' Relations with Their Mothers, Fathers, and Peers*. Chicago: University of Chicago Press, 1985.

SHMUEL SHULMAN is associate professor in the Department of Psychology at Bar Ilan University, Ramat Gan, Israel.

RACHEL LEVY-SHIFF is associate professor and head of the child clinical program in the Department of Psychology at Bar Ilan University, Ramat Gan, Israel.

PERI KEDEM is senior lecturer in the Department of Psychology at Bar Ilan University, Ramat Gan, Israel.

EITAN ALON is a graduate student in the Department of Psychology at Bar Ilan University, Ramat Gan, Israel.

This chapter focuses on developmental changes in romantic relations of adolescents differing in health status. Whereas healthy adolescents were increasingly able to balance both intimacy and conflict in their relationships with romantic partners, diabetic adolescents were unable to experience both positive and negative relationship qualities. Although this developmental delay was partly overcome, after four years some differences were still noticeable.

The Capacity to Balance Intimacy and Conflict: Differences in Romantic Relationships Between Healthy and Diabetic Adolescents

Inge Seiffge-Krenke

Dating and beginning heterosexual relationships are normative and age-typical tasks for adolescents. They spend an increasing amount of time engaging in leisure activities with members of the opposite gender (Larson and Richards, 1991) and exploring romantic relations in opposite-sex dyads (Csikszentmihalyi and Larson, 1984). The first experiences with dating and romance are undoubtedly critical to the development of adult heterosexual relationships (Furman and Wehner, 1994). However, not all adolescents are able to deal easily with dating and beginning romantic relationships, and there are great differences in the intensity and developmental speed with which adolescents approach such tasks (Cantor, Acker, and Cook-Flannagan, 1992).

In the past, much attention has been directed toward understanding the sexual aspects of adolescent romantic relationships, while the qualities of such relationships have been ignored until very recently. Consequently, existing knowledge is more of a quantitative nature. Studies have shown a progressive increase in the frequency and prominence of romantic activities, as well as systematic changes in the structure and context of opposite sex contacts (Blyth, Hill, and Thiel, 1982).

Variables that determine the onset of intercourse in heterosexual relationships have been a further area of study. The processes involved in making the transition to nonvirginity have been studied almost exclusively by North American investigators (Jessor and Jessor, 1975; Strouse and Fabes, 1987). In these studies, though, the quality of romantic relationships was of minor importance and early onset of intercourse was very much in the foreground. In Germany, there are almost no studies dealing with the psychological processes and variables determining the onset of heterosexual relationships. Above all, the studies carried out in Germany have investigated age and gender differences in the onset of heterosexual relationships and have found dramatic decreases in the age of onset of first coitus between 1970 and 1980. In a replication of Sigusch and Schmidt's (1973) study on the heterosexual activity of adolescents, Clement, Schmidt, and Kruse (1984) found that the percentage of sexually experienced eighteen-year-old males had doubled, while the percentage of experienced girls had quadrupled. In addition, Schmid-Tannwald and Urdze (1983) reported that the percentage of sexually experienced adolescents increased rapidly between the ages of fourteen and eighteen. One out of thirty fourteen-year-old girls, one out of ten fifteen-year-old girls, one out of four sixteen-year-old girls, and one out of two seventeen-year-old girls had had sexual intercourse. They also found that most adolescents had sexual intercourse regularly after the first coitus, and one year after the first intercourse, every third girl and every fourth boy was still dating the partner with whom they had had their first coitus. However, as a more recent replication by Schmidt, Klusmann, Zeitzschel, and Lange (1994) illustrates, the trend of having coitus at an even earlier age does not seem to have persisted: the rates of heterosexual activity reported in the 1970s closely match those for the 1990s.

Studies of adolescent sexual behavior in the United States also found that the age of first intercourse decreased steadily until 1980, but that this trend did not continue into the 1990s (Gagnon and others, 1989). In 1995, 50 percent of adolescents aged fifteen to nineteen had had sex, which illustrates a further drop since 1990 (Painter, 1997). Apparently, the risk of becoming infected with HIV and developing AIDS has had a marked influence on the sexual activity of adolescents, as seen in the recent tendency to delay the onset of sexual activity.

So far, little is known about the characteristics of the partner in romantic relationships, except that the first sexual intercourse is experienced nowadays at an older age than a decade ago. The perception of romantic partners has only recently become an area of interest in research. This study sets out to identify the onset of heterosexual relationships and follows their developmental course through adolescence. It also analyzes the quality of romantic relationships with respect to adolescents' characteristics, such as age, gender, and health status.

Recent theories about romantic relations have argued that romantic love entails intimacy, passion, and commitment (Sternberg, 1987). While intimacy and commitment can characterize other close relationships, passion is uniquely characteristic of romantic love. Hatfield and Rapson (1993), focusing on passionate love in particular, highlighted the presence of negative attributes. Despite the importance of romantic relationships in adolescence, they have been the subject of only limited research. In most studies, the development of intimacy was investigated. Analysis of gender differences in perceiving romantic relationships seems to indicate that females tend to focus on intimacy in relationships more than males do (Miller, 1990). Although gender differences in intimacy have been well documented (Clark-Lempers, Lempers, and Ho, 1991; Furman and Buhrmester, 1992; Furman and Wehner, 1994; Monsour, 1992; Sharabany, Gershoni, and Hofman, 1981; Werebe, 1987), it is not known when these differences first emerge. Most studies suggesting age differences in intimacy have been cross-sectional in design. They have suggested that intimacy in romantic relations increases strongly after the seventh grade, with females increasing their intimacy with boyfriends more rapidly than males with girlfriends.

The research on other important dimensions of romantic relations is sparse. Some recent research has suggested that romantic partners initially occupy a relatively low position in the adolescent hierarchy of support figures, below parents and same-sex close friends (Furman and Buhrmester, 1992). With time and experience, romantic friends gradually come to assume a more primary position in support (Furman and Wehner, 1994). Conflict and interpersonal disagreement offer further insight into the nature and processes of close relationships. It has been well documented, for example, that adolescents experience more intimacy and support but also more conflict in their relationships with mothers than, for example, with fathers (Smetana, Yau, and Hanson, 1991). As outlined by Hatfield and Rapson (1993), romantic love may entail positive characteristics such as intimacy and commitment as well as negative emotions stemming from jealousy and conflict. In fact, in an analysis of daily conflicts of fifteen- to eighteen-year-olds, Laursen (1995) found that disputes in romantic relations were third most frequent, after conflict with mothers and same-sex friends. Adolescents reported an average of one disagreement every two hours with romantic partners. The issues of conflict with romantic partners were different from those involving close friends and parents and included differences of idea or opinion, conflict over heterosexuality and friendship, and conflict over standards of behavior. It may thus be suggested that in order to maintain romantic relationships, both partners must be able to balance closeness and intimacy as well as conflict and negative emotions. Power and control are further characteristics of romantic relations that have received sparse attention in research (Stets, 1993).

Similarly, little is known about how health status influences the formation of romantic relationships and sexual experiences in adolescents. Dating and establishing romantic relationships are for many adolescents symbols of adult status, and their first sexual experiences decisively influence future behavior—for example, in their choice of partners (Hendry, Shucksmith, Love, and Glendinning, 1993). For this reason, forming the first romantic relationship is a developmental step of immense importance.

We may wonder if adolescents whose health is chronically impaired have particular difficulties in establishing romantic relationships. An analysis of the literature revealed that this topic has been sadly neglected in studies of chronically physically ill adolescents (Seiffge-Krenke and others, 1996). Except for case studies and anecdotal remarks, little has been published concerning the transition to nonvirginity in chronically ill adolescents. Even more importantly, the qualities of romantic relationships in this special group of adolescents have not been addressed so far. This is surprising because several aspects of chronic illness may impair the adolescent's ability to develop or maintain romantic relationships. For one, chronic illness is often associated with unattractive changes in physical appearance. In addition, management of the chronic illness also affects the adolescent's general lifestyle: leisure activities may be restricted and daily routines are often interrupted (La Greca, 1990).

This study focuses on diabetes, a chronic illness with a comparably high prevalence in adolescence (Ahmed and Ahmed, 1985). Relative to other chronic diseases, such as arthritis or cancer, diabetes places few restrictions on adolescents, who are able to participate in nearly all leisure activities. Although the diabetic adolescent may not show overt signs of being afflicted by the disease, the demands of diabetes management nevertheless require that the adolescent constantly exercise self-control, for example, in observing dietary restrictions or in monitoring glycemic control, thus hindering spontaneity. Also, the diabetic adolescent's daily activities are interrupted by blood sugar tests and insulin injections. Meeting these demands may disturb intimate interactions with romantic partners. Moreover, the diabetic adolescent can participate in typical teenagers' activities, such as eating junk food, experimenting with alcohol consumption, or taking vacations with romantic partners, only if he or she accepts the health risks or takes special precautions. It is suggested that these issues may become areas of conflict in diabetics' romantic relations. Nathan and Goetz (1984) pointed out that diabetic adolescents' intensive self-centeredness also could adversely affect relationships with romantic partners. To achieve a stable metabolism, diabetic adolescents must significantly increase their attention to physical processes. This strong preoccupation with the self is necessary for the diabetic adolescent's survival, but can hinder his or her ability to show the empathy needed for close, satisfying, and intimate relationships.

Research Questions

We may thus ask if chronically ill adolescents are able to balance positive and negative aspects in their romantic relationships and if the quality of their romantic relationships equals the quality of those experienced by healthy adolescents. This question was addressed by comparing healthy and diabetic adolescents' perceptions of the qualities of their romantic relationships. More specifically, how adolescents perceived their relationships to romantic partners in general and how they experienced current dyadic relationships with romantic partners were examined. Although other dimensions of relationships were of interest, the focus was particularly on intimacy and conflict and their development in relation to age, gender, and health status. Because actual experiences in romantic relations may shape adolescents' perceptions, the study began by determining and analyzing formal characteristics of romantic relationships, such as age of onset of heterosexual relationships as well as number and change of partners. Next, the adolescents were asked what they liked best about their current romantic partners and what they generally thought was important in romantic relationships. Then the quality of their relationships with romantic partners was analyzed using more standardized methods. The results obtained by two research methods—self-reports provided in interviews focusing on global and dyadic aspects of romantic relationships, and standardized questionnaires—have been integrated. A longitudinal design was selected, allowing the comparison of developmental gains and losses in both groups.

Method

Subjects. One hundred and ninety-eight adolescents participated in the study, which entailed four annual surveys. All subjects resided in Germany. At the first survey in 1991, the mean age of the adolescents was 13.9 years, and at the fourth survey in 1994 it was 17.1 years. The gender ratio was balanced for both groups for all four surveys. Almost half of the adolescents suffered from insulin-dependent diabetes mellitus (N = 91, 46 males and 45 females), and 107 were healthy (46 males and 61 females). At the beginning of the investigation, the adolescents were in the sixth and seventh grades in German high schools, and at the end they were in grades 10 and 11. Most of the adolescents came from intact middle-class families. The two groups did not differ significantly with respect to social class, age, occupation, and marital status of the parents, or number of siblings. Eighty-one percent of the adolescents were raised in two-parent families, 19 percent were raised in single-parent or divorced families. The average number of children per family was 1.6. The mean level of parents' education was 12.3 years for fathers and 11.8 years for mothers.

At the beginning of the study, the adolescents in the diabetic sample had been ill for a mean of 5.4 years. Glycosylated hemoglobin (HbA_1)-values served as a medical criterion for the quality of adaptation to the illness. At the first survey, 24 percent of the diabetics were well adapted ($HbA_1 < 7.6$), 45 percent had achieved a medium level of adaptation ($HbA_1 = 7.6$ to 9.5) and 31 percent had adapted poorly ($HbA_1 > 9.5$). Thus 69 percent of the adolescents had satisfactory to good metabolic control, which remained fairly stable over the following years.

Measures. The Network of Relationship Inventory (NRI) developed by Furman and Buhrmester (1985) was administered. It assesses the following eleven dimensions of romantic relations: companionship, conflict, instrumental aid, satisfaction, intimacy, nurturance, affection, punishment, admiration, relative power, and reliable alliance. These dimensions may be classified according to two general dimensions, namely, social support and negative interaction. Each of the eleven relationship dimensions was assessed by three items. The subjects indicated on a standard five-point Likert-type scale to what extent each attribute was experienced in relationships with romantic friends (from 1 = little or none, to 5 = the most). Internal consistency coefficients (Cronbach alphas) were calculated for each of the eleven scales. The mean alpha coefficients were as follows: companionship, .88; conflict, .79; instrumental aid, .80; satisfaction, .81; intimacy, .82; nurturance, .76; affection, .87; punishment, .73; admiration, .76; relative power, .86; and reliable alliance, .81.

In addition, the adolescents took part in semistructured interviews in which they were asked about romantic relationships on both global and dyadic levels. At the global level, adolescents were asked to talk about romantic partners in general; at the dyadic level, they were asked to talk about their current romantic relationships. The researchers inquired about how they had met their partners, how long they had been dating them, what they did together, what they especially liked about their boyfriend or girlfriend, what kind of conflicts existed, whether they had had sexual relations with the partner, and how seriously they took the relationship. Furthermore, they were asked about their first experience with sexual intercourse, and whether they had had sexual relationships with other partners. In the following years they were asked whether they still dated the same partner; if not, what the reason was for ending the relationship; and if they currently had a romantic partner.

Procedure. Before each survey, we contacted each participant and arranged a date for the interview. Each summer from 1991 to 1994, we visited the adolescents in their homes and conducted the interviews. At the end of each interview, we asked the adolescent to fill out the NRI.

Results

Overview of the Analysis. The adolescents' responses in the interview were coded by two raters. The concordance coefficients were determined by Kappa. In regard to general perceptions of relationships ("Generally speaking, what is important to you in romantic relations?"), the Kappa amounted to $K = .87$, $p < .001$. At the dyadic level, the concordance coefficients amounted to $K = .73$, $p < .001$ for the twelve questions concerning romantic relations. The cross-sectional analysis of the interview data was conducted using chi^2-tests of independence and Kendall's tau. The Cochran Test was used separately for the longitudinal analysis of nominally scaled interview data for healthy and diabetic adolescents.

The main question addressed in this study concerned the differences in perceptions of romantic relationships in diabetic and healthy adolescents. Means and standard deviations of the eleven relationship dimensions of the NRI, as well as the two general dimensions, social support and negative interaction, were determined. Changes over time were analyzed by MANOVAs of repeated measurements, with time as a within-subject factor and health status (ill/healthy) as a between-subject factor, including the data from all four waves of the NRI. Repeated measurement MANOVAs included a Greenhouse-Geisser correction for variance heterogeneity. Due to their central importance of relationships in adolescence, the NRI relationship dimensions intimacy and conflict were subjected to further detailed analysis with respect to the variables age, gender, and health status by 2 (health status) $\times$ 2 (gender) $\times$ 4 (time) MANOVAs.

Beginning Heterosexual Relationships. In the first year of the survey (when our subjects were about thirteen years old), very few adolescents of the total sample had a boyfriend or girlfriend, but this number increased distinctly over the second and third years of the study. The increase was much more rapid in healthy adolescents than in chronically ill adolescents (in 1991: diabetics 1 percent, healthy 4 percent; in 1992: diabetics 2 percent, healthy 14 percent; in 1993: diabetics 8 percent, healthy 22 percent; and in 1994: diabetics 11 percent, healthy 36 percent). The interview data revealed that the mere idea of heterosexual relationships, even before such relationships had been experienced, was mentioned seven times more often by healthy adolescents than by the chronically ill. Dealing with heterosexual relationships and with problems in finding a partner was mentioned increasingly by the healthy group between the first and second surveys, and these topics continued especially to concern them up to the last survey. In the fourth survey, many more healthy than ill adolescents considered not yet having a boyfriend or girlfriend to be a deficit. These results illustrate that relationships with the opposite gender—in reality or fantasy—seem to be of minor importance to diabetics.

By the fourth wave, when the adolescents were about seventeen years old, the sexually experienced adolescents reported having had a total mean number of 2.8 sexual partners (SD = 1.3), with healthy adolescents reporting higher numbers of sexual partners than diabetic adolescents. The majority of sexually experienced diabetic adolescents had had sexual relations with only one partner during the four years. It is important to note that very few diabetic adolescents had sexual relations without a steady relationship; the percentage of their healthy peers who had sexual relations without having a steady boyfriend or girlfriend was eight times higher.

It is also striking that healthy and chronically ill adolescents seemed to become acquainted with their romantic partners in different social settings. Diabetic adolescents frequently stated that they had met their partners while engaged in leisure time activities with their parents, such as during family vacations, or in organized leisure-time institutions, such as summer camps. In contrast, healthy adolescents became acquainted with their partners through their clique of friends. No differences were found between ill and healthy adolescents concerning other characteristics of romantic relationships, such as time period of dating, common activities, frequency of dates, or seriousness of relationships.

Characteristics of Romantic Partners and Activities Together. When asked what they liked best about their boyfriend or girlfriend, healthy and ill adolescents named similar characteristics, but with varying frequencies. In the fourth wave, for example, healthy adolescents named personality characteristics more often than ill adolescents (healthy, 48 percent; diabetic, 39 percent); similar differences were seen for the categories intimacy (healthy, 46 percent; diabetic, 27 percent), attractiveness (healthy, 25 percent; diabetic, 11 percent), and similar interests (healthy, 32 percent; diabetic, 21 percent). The diabetics surpassed their healthy coevals in naming the categories emotional support (diabetic, 22 percent; healthy, 17 percent) and instrumental aid (diabetic, 12 percent; healthy, 2 percent). Other significant differences between healthy and chronically ill adolescents were found in their responses to the question, "Generally speaking, what is important to you in romantic relationships?" The results of the fourth wave illustrate these differences. On a global level, chronically ill adolescents found it more important than healthy adolescents that romantic partners be good listeners (diabetic, 12 percent; healthy, 5 percent), join them in carrying out everyday activities (diabetic, 10 percent; healthy, 4 percent), and show understanding (diabetic, 26 percent; healthy, 14 percent). In contrast, healthy adolescents stated more often than diabetics that having fun together (healthy, 8 percent; diabetic, 1 percent) and sharing activities (healthy, 16 percent; diabetic, 2 percent) were more important.

Healthy adolescents were also more willing to mention sources of conflicts with their heterosexual partners. Table 4.1 displays the frequencies of different sources of conflict in romantic relations, as reported by diabetic and healthy adolescents at the fourth wave, that is, at the age of about seventeen years. As can be seen in the table, rivalry, jealousy, and power relations were frequent sources of conflict in the romantic relationships of healthy adolescents. Lack of sufficient attention was one reason for conflict named frequently by diabetics but less often by healthy adolescents.

Differences in Perceptions of Romantic Relationships. Table 4.2 displays the means and standard deviations of the NRI scales for healthy and diabetic adolescents separately, across the four measurement points.

Effect of Health Status. Significant differences in the NRI between healthy and ill adolescents were found in four of the eleven subscales. Whereas the healthy adolescents' satisfaction with their heterosexual relationships, $F(1, 27) = 18.21, p < .001$, and their intimacy in romantic relations, $F(1, 27) = 12.96, p < .001$, was higher for all four measurement points, ill adolescents

Table 4.1. Sources of Conflict in Romantic Relations Reported by Diabetic and Healthy Adolescents (f percent) at Wave 4, 1994

	Diabetic	Healthy
Closeness/intimacy	5.9	5.1
Jealousy/rivalry	5.9	28.1
Power relations	11.8	15.6
Unacceptable behaviors	11.7	9.4
Lack of sufficient attention	35.3	18.6
Avoidance of conflict	17.6	10.6

Table 4.2. Means and Standard Deviations of Relationship Quality with Romantic Partners as Perceived by Diabetic and Healthy Adolescents at Each Time of Measurement

NRI Romantic Partners	Time 1 M	(SD)	Time 2 M	(SD)	Time 3 M	(SD)	Time 4 M	(SD)
Companionship								
Diabetic	10.33	(3.79)	11.18	(4.12)	12.17	(4.39)	12.33	(3.96)
Healthy	8.29	(5.34)	11.16	(4.00)	12.13	(3.52)	11.79	(3.13)
Conflict								
Diabetic	4.25	(2.04)	4.90	(3.68)	5.30	(3.41)	5.99	(2.80)
Healthy	5.80	(2.02)	6.20	(1.33)	5.50	(1.34)	6.10	(2.43)
Instrumental Aid								
Diabetic	8.22	(3.42)	10.44	(2.19)	10.99	(2.93)	11.30	(2.21)
Healthy	6.90	(4.17)	9.00	(2.35)	8.35	(2.50)	8.37	(2.21)
Satisfaction								
Diabetic	10.46	(4.06)	11.20	(3.96)	12.18	(3.49)	12.82	(2.96)
Healthy	9.86	(4.61)	10.35	(2.99)	11.48	(3.84)	11.71	(3.56)
Intimacy								
Diabetic	9.67	(4.82)	11.44	(3.88)	12.22	(3.31)	13.02	(3.14)
Healthy	8.02	(4.66)	11.75	(2.59)	12.05	(2.96)	12.45	(3.72)
Nurturance								
Diabetic	8.27	(3.23)	8.79	(2.88)	9.91	(3.11)	10.64	(2.77)
Healthy	7.73	(4.26)	10.33	(3.96)	11.36	(3.53)	11.46	(2.94)
Affection								
Diabetic	9.89	(3.76)	13.00	(2.35)	12.44	(2.65)	13.33	(2.83)
Healthy	9.58	(4.88)	12.68	(2.06)	12.53	(2.74)	12.26	(2.90)
Punishment								
Diabetic	3.91	(1.45)	3.15	(1.02)	3.27	(1.45)	3.09	(.89)
Healthy	3.27	(1.16)	3.98	(1.12)	4.00	(1.57)	4.27	(1.86)
Admiration								
Diabetic	8.55	(3.45)	9.13	(3.00)	10.27	(2.27)	10.55	(2.98)
Healthy	7.36	(4.02)	9.36	(3.11)	10.32	(3.19)	10.27	(3.02)
Relative Power								
Diabetic	7.67	(2.59)	6.89	(2.62)	5.00	(1.80)	6.33	(2.06)
Healthy	7.88	(2.34)	7.00	(1.46)	7.06	(2.56)	7.29	(2.39)
Reliable Alliance								
Diabetic	10.46	(3.36)	10.21	(3.01)	10.00	(3.61)	11.00	(3.09)
Healthy	7.77	(4.57)	9.29	(2.98)	10.32	(3.59)	10.27	(3.60)

consistently experienced higher companionship, $F(1, 27) = 4.18$, $p < .05$, and instrumental aid, $F(1, 27) = 5.60$, $p < .05$. Significant effects of health status were also found in the two major dimensions, social support, $F(1,27) = 3.14$, $p < .05$, and negative interaction, $F(1,27) = 2.96$, $p = .05$, illustrating higher values for healthy than for ill adolescents.

Change over Time. In several of the eleven NRI dimensions, time effects existed for both groups. Companionship, $F(3, 81) = 5.30$, $p < .01$, intimacy, $F(3, 81) = 7.68$, $p < .001$, nurturance, $F(3, 78) = 8.21$, $p < .001$, affection, $F(3, 79) = 7.31$, $p < .001$, and admiration, $F(3, 80) = 4.84$, $p < .01$, increased significantly over four years. In summary, positive relationship dimensions, added to the general dimension social support, significantly increased in both groups over time, $F(3, 81) = 4.45$, $p < .05$. Only one relationship dimension, relative power, $F(3, 77) = 2.53$, $p = .06$, showed a tendency to decrease over time in both groups.

Interaction Between Health Status and Time. Several interaction effects between health status and time were found, indicating different courses of development in diabetics and healthy adolescents. Negative interaction as a general dimension, $F(3, 79) = 3.34$, $p < .05$, as well as punishment as a single dimension, $F(3, 80) = 3.79$, $p < .05$, increased in healthy adolescents over time, while the scores decreased or remained stable in diabetics. Over time the ill adolescents showed an increase and the healthy adolescents a decrease in their respective scores for instrumental aid, $F(3, 81) = 4.05$, $p < .05$. In contrast, the importance of reliable alliance, $F(1, 57) = 7.21$, $p < .001$, grew for healthy adolescents but did not change for diabetics.

Intimacy and Conflict as a Function of Age, Gender, and Health Status. This section focuses on findings concerning two central characteristics of close relationships in adolescence: intimacy and conflict. The results reported so far showed that intimacy in romantic relationships of adolescents with different health status increased over four years. However, compared to chronically ill adolescents, healthy subjects had significantly higher scores for intimacy at all four measurement points. In contrast, the scores for conflict in romantic relations reported by healthy and diabetic adolescents remained stable over time.

To test the hypothesis that intimacy and conflict in romantic relationships vary according to age, gender, and health status, a 2×2 (health status $\times$ gender) repeated measurement MANOVA was conducted for intimacy and conflict values of the NRI for romantic friends. The results showed that females expressed significantly greater intimacy toward their romantic partners than males, $F(1, 25) = 9.80$, $p < .001$, and that in general intimacy in romantic relationships increased with age, $F(3, 75) = 9.10$, $p < .001$. A significant interaction effect of health status and gender was found, $F(1, 25) = 4.91$, $p < .05$. Regarding conflicts in romantic relations, however, no significant effect of age or gender was found; however, a tendency emerged for more conflict reported by healthy adolescents of both gender, $F(1,42) = 2.59$, $p = .10$.

Figure 4.1 illustrates intimacy development in romantic relationships for male and female healthy and diabetic adolescents. Males and females from both groups increased their intimacy in romantic relationships over time; however, the differences between the genders and between ill and healthy subjects remained notable. As can be seen, there were increasing discrepancies between diabetic males and females with respect to the development of intimacy in romantic relationships. The different developmental speed in healthy adolescents' levels of intimacy with romantic partners resulted also in a growing discrepancy between males' and females' perceived relations to their romantic partners. The level of intimacy reported by diabetic females at the beginning

Figure 4.1. Intimacy Perceived in Romantic Relations Depending on Gender and Health Status

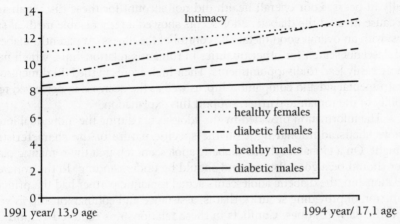

of the investigation was already remarkably high. It is worth noting that they showed the strongest gains over time.

Discussion

In a longitudinal study on an early adolescent sample, the formal characteristics of romantic relationships were analyzed and related to the more qualitative changes over the course of four years, as most of the subjects approached late adolescence. Perceived romantic relationships served as a key dimension for understanding the transition to romantic love. The most important findings were the marked differences in formal characteristics and in perception of romantic relationships in adolescents as a function of health status. The age of onset of heterosexual relationships in healthy adolescents found in this study closely paralleled the findings reported in other studies (see Anderson Darling, Davidson, and Passarello, 1992; Schmidt, Klusmann, Zeitzschel, and Lange, 1994). However, the diabetic adolescents started to have heterosexual relationships later and were less sexually active. More importantly, romantic relationships seemed to serve different functions in diabetic and healthy adolescents.

How can the delay in the onset of sexual intercourse of diabetic adolescents and the specific qualities of their romantic relationships be explained? First, it must be emphasized that the chronically ill adolescents showed no objective deficits of physical maturity; their levels of physical maturation corresponded to the norms of their ages. No significant differences were found between the two groups with respect to age of menarche and semenarche (see Seiffge-Krenke and others, 1996). Thus differences in physical maturation do not appear to be responsible for diabetics' delay in beginning or lower rates of increase of heterosexual relations. At the time of the fourth survey, when the adolescents were about seventeen years old, the rate of sexual activity in healthy adolescents was already three times higher than that of their chronically ill peers. Poor overall health did not account for these discrepancies, because most of the diabetic adolescents showed a rather stable medical status, with an overall good metabolic control of the illness. Apparently, diabetic adolescents search for other qualities in romantic relationships, which may more easily lead to disappointments. Their high scores in the NRI dimensions instrumental aid and companionship, as well as the decrease in perceived reliability of the romantic partner, support this explanation.

The information provided by the adolescents during the individual interviews sheds additional light on the specific nature of the characteristics sought. On a global level, the diabetic adolescent felt that the romantic partner should be a good listener and should be understanding. In the concrete relationship, the diabetic adolescent's actual romantic partner had the primary function of providing security, that is, assistance and companionship in very specific daily routines. Conflicts in these relationships centered around the diabetics' feelings that they lacked sufficient attention from their partners. Further, diabetic adolescents were unwilling to date others while in a steady relationship. Diabetics thus looked for partners who could offer them more security, support, and assistance, as well as more harmonious understanding, than their healthy peers sought. The relationship with romantic partners seemed to be less balanced and more demanding, compared to romantic relations in healthy peers.

As key dimensions for romantic relationships, intimacy and conflict development in both healthy and diabetic males and females were analyzed. Although initially low, intimacy in romantic relationships increased dramatically over time for all groups investigated. This trend toward increasing intimacy in romantic relationships with increasing age has already been demonstrated in cross-sectional studies (Sharabany, Gershoni, and Hofman, 1981). The present study's longitudinal data also confirmed the existence of marked gender differences in intimacy, as seen in several other studies (Buhrmester and Furman, 1987; Moore and Rosenthal, 1993; Sanderson and Cantor, 1995). In the present study, females reported higher levels of intimacy in romantic relationships than did males, irrespective of health status. Moreover, increasing discrepancies in intimacy in romantic relationships were perceived by male and female diabetics. Starting from an already comparably high level, female diabetics' perception of intimacy in romantic relations increased rapidly. Male diabetics' perceived level of intimacy, initially much lower, also showed a strong increase. Nevertheless, it must be emphasized that despite this gain, the male diabetics' level of intimacy did not reach that reported by their healthy peers. An analysis of conflict in romantic relations did reveal only a tendentious main effect of health status, with healthy adolescents experiencing more conflicts in romantic relations than diabetics. However, negative interaction in romantic relationships increased more over time in healthy adolescents than in chronically ill adolescents.

While integrating these findings into a broader conceptual framework that encompasses other relationship dimensions, it has to be stressed that the increase shown over time by healthy adolescents in both positive (social support) and negative (negative interaction) relationship dimensions of the NRI was not characteristic of diabetic adolescents. More specifically, diabetic adolescents of both genders did not perceive their romantic relationships as positively as healthy adolescents did. Although the diabetic adolescents' appreciation for their romantic partners' instrumental aid increased over the course of four years, satisfaction with the relationship and its reliable alliance did not improve. Perceived conflict in romantic relations also remained stable. By contrast, healthy adolescents' relations to romantic partners were marked by increased levels of intimacy over time, as well as by more frequent conflicts and negative interactions. These results thus suggest that diabetic adolescents were not capable of simultaneously experiencing both positive and negative qualities in their relationships, which were mainly characterized by receiving instrumental aid.

An examination of conflict issues further indicates distinct concerns associated with conflicts in the romantic relationships of diabetics as compared to healthy adolescents. The disagreements over power structure and jealousy found in healthy adolescents reflect a growing emphasis on relationship equality, intimacy, and exclusivity. The ill subjects' comparatively high number of conflicts centering around a lack of sufficient attention suggests that romantic relations in diabetics may serve different functions than in healthy adolescents. Sanderson and Cantor (1995) have recently argued that adolescents differ with respect to the goals they pursue in heterosexual relationships. Some adolescents focus on achieving and maintaining intimacy, that is, closeness and trust, in their heterosexual relationships; for others, romantic relationships serve the goal of establishing identity. However, the fusion of both goals is important, that is, an independent identity must be developed and this identity must be merged with others in intimate relations. The results of the present study demonstrate that chronically ill adolescents, possibly because of the intense self-focusing that is necessary for illness management, lack empathy and intimacy with their romantic partners. Especially in early and mid adolescence, romantic relations in diabetic adolescents are reminiscent of the model of a caring mother and a demanding child, and have not yet reached a mature stage in which closeness and conflict are balanced. Nevertheless, longitudinal analyses indicated that diabetic adolescents achieved gains in several major relationship dimensions and tried to balance out their deficits in important aspects of romantic relationships.

References

Ahmed, P. I., and Ahmed, N. (eds.). *Coping with Juvenile Diabetes.* Springfield, Ill.: Thomas, 1985.

Anderson Darling, C., Davidson, J. K., and Passarello, L. C. "The Mystique of First Intercourse Among College Youth: The Role of Partners, Contraceptions, and Psychological Reactions." *Journal of Youth and Adolescence,* 1992, *21,* 97–117.

Blyth, D. A., Hill, J. P., and Thiel, K. S. "Early Adolescent Significant Others: Grade and Gender Differences in Perceived Relationships with Familiar and Nonfamiliar Adults and Young People." *Journal of Youth and Adolescence,* 1982, *11,* 425–449.

Buhrmester, D., and Furman, W. "The Development of Companionship and Intimacy." *Child Development,* 1987, *58,* 1101–1113.

Cantor, N., Acker, M., and Cook-Flannagan, C. "Conflicts and Preoccupation in the Intimacy Life Task." *Journal of Personality and Social Psychology,* 1992, *63,* 644–655.

Clark-Lempers, D. S., Lempers, J. D., and Ho, C. "Early, Middle and Late Adolescents' Perceptions of Their Relationships with Significant Others." *Journal of Adolescent Research,* 1991, *6,* 296–315.

Clement, U., Schmidt, G., and Kruse, M. "Changes in Sex Differences in Sexual Behavior: A Replication of a Study on West German Students." *Archives of Sexual Behavior,* 1984, *13,* 99–120.

Csikszentmihalyi, M., and Larson, R. *Being Adolescent: Conflict and Growth in the Teenage Years.* New York: Basic Books, 1984.

Furman, W., and Buhrmester, D. "Children's Perception of the Personal Relationships in Their Social Networks." *Developmental Psychology,* 1985, *21,* 1016–1024.

Furman, W., and Buhrmester, D. "Age and Sex Differences in Perceptions of Networks of Personal Relationships." *Child Development,* 1992, *63,* 103–115.

Furman, W., and Wehner, E. A. "Romantic Views: Toward a Theory of Adolescent Romantic Relationships." In R. Montemayor, G. Adams, and G. Gulotta (eds.), *Advances in Adolescent Development.* Personal Relationships During Adolescence, no. 3. Thousand Oaks, Calif.: Sage, 1994.

Gagnon, J., Lindenbaum, S., Martin, J. L., May, R. M., Menken, J., Turner, C. F., and Zabin, L. S. "Sexual Behavior and AIDS." In C. F. Turner, H. G. Miller, and J. E. Moses (eds.), *AIDS, Sexual Behavior and Intravenous Drug-Use.* Washington, D.C.: National Academy Press, 1989.

Hatfield, E., and Rapson, R. "Love and Attachment Processes." In M. Lewis and J. Haviland (eds.), *Handbook of Emotions.* New York: Guilford Press, 1993.

Hendry, L. B., Shucksmith, J., Love, J. G., and Glendinning, A. *Young People's Leisure and Lifestyles.* London: Routledge, 1993.

Jessor, R., and Jessor, S. L. "Transition from Virginity to Nonvirginity Among Youth: A Social-Psychological Study over Time." *Developmental Psychology,* 1975, *11,* 473–484.

La Greca, A. M. "Social Consequences of Pediatric Conditions: Fertile Area of Future Investigation and Intervention?" *Journal of Pediatric Psychology,* 1990, *15,* 285–307.

Larson, R., and Richards, M. H. "Daily Companionship in Late Childhood and Early Adolescence: Changing Developmental Contexts." *Child Development,* 1991, *62,* 284–300.

Laursen, B. "Conflict and Social Interaction in Adolescent Relationships." *Journal of Research on Adolescence,* 1995, *5,* 55–70.

Miller, K. E. "Adolescents' Same-Sex and Opposite-Sex Peer Relations: Sex Differences in Popularity, Perceived Social Competence, and Social Cognitive Skills." *Journal of Adolescent Research,* 1990, *5,* 222–241.

Monsour, M. "Meanings of Intimacy in Cross-and Same-Sex Friendships." *Journal of Social and Personal Relationships,* 1992, *9,* 277–295.

Moore, S., and Rosenthal, D. *Sexuality in Adolescence.* London: Routledge, 1993.

Nathan, S. W., and Goetz, P. "Psychosocial Aspects of Chronic Illness: Group Interactions in Diabetic Girls." *Children's Health Care,* 1984, *13,* 24–30.

Painter, K. "Fewer Teens Having Sex; More Use Birth Control." *USA Today,* May 2, 1997.

Sanderson, C. A., and Cantor, N. "Social Dating in Late Adolescence: Implications for Safer Sexual Activity." *Journal of Personality and Social Psychology,* 1995, *68,* 1121–1134.

Schmid-Tannwald, I., and Urdze, A. *Sexualität und Kontrazeption aus der Sicht der Jugendlichen und ihren Eltern* [Sexuality and Contraception in the View of Adolescents and Their Parents]. Stuttgart, Germany: Kohlhammer, 1983.

Schmidt, G., Klusmann, D., Zeitzschel, U., and Lange, C. "Changes in Adolescents' Sexuality Between 1970 and 1990 in West-Germany." *Archives of Sexual Behavior*, 1994, *23*, 489–513.

Seiffge-Krenke, I., Boeger, A., Schmidt, C., Kollmar, F., Floss, A., and Roth, M. *Chronisch kranke Jugendliche und ihre Familien: Belastung, Bewältigung und psychosoziale Folgen* [Chronically Ill Adolescents and Their Families: Stress, Coping and Psychosocial Adaptation]. Stuttgart, Germany: Kohlhammer, 1996.

Sharabany, R., Gershoni, R., and Hofman, J. E. "Girlfriend, Boyfriend: Age and Sex Differences in Intimate Friendship." *Developmental Psychology*, 1981, *17*, 800–808.

Sigusch, K., and Schmidt, G. *Jugendsexualität* [Adolescent Sexuality]. Stuttgart, Germany: Enke, 1973.

Smetana, J. G., Yau, J., and Hanson, S. "Conflict Resolution in Families with Adolescents." *Journal of Research on Adolescence*, 1991, *1*, 189–206.

Sternberg, R. "Liking Versus Loving: A Comparative Evaluation of Theories." *Psychological Bulletin*, 1987, *102*, 331–345.

Stets, J. E. "Control in Dating Relationships." *Journal of Marriage and the Family*, 1993, *55*, 673–685.

Strouse, J. S., and Fabes, R. A. "A Conceptualization of Transition to Nonvirginity in Adolescent Females." *Journal of Adolescent Research*, 1987, *2*, 332–348.

Werebe, M. J. "Friendship and Dating Relationships Among French Adolescents." *Journal of Adolescence*, 1987, *10*, 268–289.

INGE SEIFFGE-KRENKE is professor of psychology and head of the developmental section in the Department of Psychology, University of Mainz, Germany.

Romantic relationships emerge in a context of earlier experiences with caregivers and peers that contribute to variability in adolescents' capacities for intimacy.

Developmental Precursors of Romantic Relationships: A Longitudinal Analysis

W. Andrew Collins, Katherine C. Hennighausen, David Taylor Schmit, L. Alan Sroufe

Among the popular stereotypes of adolescence, images of romantic and sexual awakening loom large. In both fiction and autobiography, writers invoke the raging hormones, "first loves," and distinctly more romantic interests of the teenage years. These common impressions accord with empirical findings that behaviors associated with romantic interests (such as dating and sexual activity) increase during the teenage years (for reviews, see Katchadourian, 1990; Savin-Williams, in press; Zani, 1993). From a developmental perspective, however, the romantic experiences of adolescents represent one phase of a meaningful progression of relationships across age periods (Collins and Sroufe, in press). Early caregiver-child relationships, peer relationships in preschool and middle childhood, and friendships in adolescence contribute to adolescents' functioning in teenage romantic relationships.

Several assumptions about relationships underlie the developmental view adopted in this chapter. The first assumption is that all types of relationships in all periods of life have certain core features in common. Even though with development changes occur in the types of relationships that are central and in relationship capacities, interpersonal relating in successive life periods builds on prior relationship experiences. Second, relationships are not simply the sum of personal characteristics of each member of the dyad; rather, relationships are the unique patterning and qualities of dyadic interactions that endure over time (Hinde and Stevenson-Hinde, 1987; Sroufe and Fleeson, 1986). Third, individuals and relationships are both the products and the architects of the relationships in which they participate (Sroufe, 1989; Sroufe and Fleeson, 1986). Fourth, relationships are integral to competence, defined as "the ability to make effective use of personal and environmental resources to achieve a good developmental outcome" (Waters and Sroufe, 1983, p. 81). "Good" developmental outcomes are those that lead to healthy adaptations with regard to the salient issues of later developmental phases, or at least that do not limit or foreclose on important developmental changes (Elicker, Englund, and Sroufe, 1992; Sroufe and Fleeson, 1986).

A salient issue underlying healthy romantic relationships during adolescence is a capacity for intimacy. This capacity is similar to, yet distinct from, the preadolescent issue of forming close mutual relationships. With time, satisfying friendships, and eventually romantic relationships, involve not only mutually self-disclosing behaviors but also experiences of feeling understood, validated, and cared for (Reis and Shaver, 1988).

The premise of this chapter is that differences among adolescents' behavior in romantic relationships are embedded in both earlier and concurrent relationship experiences that foster the development of a capacity for intimacy. The chapter is divided into four sections. The first section outlines a developmental view of romantic relationships. The second section summarizes findings from a twenty-year longitudinal study based on this view, with particular attention to links between relationships with parents and interactions with peers prior to adolescence that set the stage for close relationships during adolescence. Particular attention is given to the implications of counternormative behavior with peers in middle childhood. The third section reports new evidence that these preadolescent relationships are precursors of romantic relationships during adolescence. The fourth section proposes some criteria for conducting future research on the development of romantic relationships during adolescence.

A Developmental View of the Transition to Romantic Relationships

Central to our view of the emergence and nature of romantic relationships during adolescence is the idea that children form expectations concerning themselves in the environment based on salient relationship experiences in earlier life (see, for example, Bowlby, 1973; Sroufe and Fleeson, 1986). These expectations guide encounters with the environment and interpretations of experience (Zeanah and Zeanah, 1989). Children who have positive expectations concerning others, feelings of worth and confidence, and conceptions of relationships as responsive and mutually engaging behave toward peers in positive ways. These children expect and elicit positive and age-appropriate support from adults and stretch their abilities in setting goals and meeting challenges. Other persons commonly react in complementary ways (Sroufe, Carlson, and Shulman, 1993; Waters, Kondo-Ikemura, Posada, and Richters, 1991). In successive developmental periods, this continuous, transactional process perpetuates the child's interpersonal expectations, albeit in new forms and in new contexts (Sroufe and Fleeson, 1986; Waters, Kondo-Ikemura, Posada, and Richters, 1991).

The capacity for intimacy evolves from earlier interpersonal capacities through a series of transformations, each of which is built on the previous ones. Thus adolescents' abilities to form and maintain relationships, including romantic attachments, in the face of an increasingly larger and more diverse set of social experiences reflect their experiences in relationships from infancy onward. Although the expansion and more extensive differentiation of social networks during adolescence makes it more difficult to discern linkages across time, understanding how the capacity for intimacy grows in each period of development provides important clues to how and why romantic relationships may vary during adolescence.

Normative Precursors of Later Romantic Relationships

This view of developmental precursors to romantic relationships has been shaped by experiences in the Minnesota Parent-Child Project, in which 190 first-born individuals have been studied since the third trimester of the mother's pregnancy (see Egeland and Brunnquell, 1979, for an early report). Infants and/or mothers were seen seven times in the child's first year, twice in each of the next three years, yearly though grade 4, and five times from age twelve to age nineteen. Assessments included neurological status; motor, cognitive, and intellectual development; maternal personality and IQ; parent-child interaction; temperament; peer relationships; personality development; and contextual variables such as life stress and social support. Children were observed in home, laboratory, and school. In addition, subsamples of these participants have been studied intensively in a semester-long nursery school program, in a four-week summer camp at age ten, and in a weekend retreat at age fifteen. These subsamples were representative of the sample at large.

The primary measure of early relationships was the Strange Situation procedure (Ainsworth, Blehar, Waters, and Wall, 1978). This twenty-minute procedure involves a series of episodes with primary caregiver, infant, and an adult stranger in a playroom. Based on behavior in the Strange Situation, Ainsworth identified *secure attachment* with use of the caregiver as a secure base for exploration, and a pattern of emotional responses to separation and reunion that indicates confidence in the accessibility and responsiveness of the caregiver. In a second, contrasting pattern, termed *anxious/resistant attachment,* the relationship does not serve the infant as a secure base. Infants have difficulty exploring even when the caregiver is present; moreover, they become quite upset by the separation episodes and show great difficulty settling upon reunion, even when in contact with the caregiver. In the third pattern, called *anxious/avoidant attachment,* children commonly show little distress during the separations, and upon reunion they ignore, turn or move away from, or show abortive approaches to their caregivers. Again, the relationship does not serve as a support for exploration following the stress of separation.

Secure attachments would likely be more conducive than the two insecure patterns to the subsequent development of a capacity for intimacy, for several reasons. First, relationships in which caregivers are readily available and responsive to the child should lead to positive expectancies about the reliability of others as resources for the child. Second, an empathic, responsive caregiver provides firsthand experience in the nature of empathic relating generally (Sroufe and Fleeson, 1986). Third, responsive care and support for autonomy enhances the individual's sense of self-worth and self-efficacy, which in turn underlie characteristics that are likely to be attractive to future partners (such as self-confidence, curiosity, enthusiasm, and positive affect) (Elicker, Englund, and Sroufe, 1992). Much research has documented impressive relations between early caregiver-child relationships and later key relationships, and between both these earlier and later patterns and friendships in which intimacy can occur in adolescence (see, for example, Elicker, Englund, and Sroufe, 1992; Shulman, Elicker, and Sroufe, 1994). The following findings illustrate these links.

During preschool, children with secure histories were more popular with peers. These children also participated more actively in the peer group and manifested more positive affect and less negative affect in their encounters than insecurely attached children (Sroufe, 1983). Children with anxious-avoidant attachment histories were not only significantly less competent in all of these respects, but were also more aggressive in the classroom. Those with anxious/resistant attachment were easily frustrated and sought contact with teachers more than with peers (Sroufe, 1983). Moreover, children with early histories of secure attachment displayed greater reciprocity and dealt more effectively with conflicts in interactions with preschool peers (Liberman, 1977). When we focused on specific pairs of children who played together frequently, pairs containing at least one avoidant member formed relationships that were less deep (less characterized by mutuality, responsiveness, and affective involvement) and more hostile than the other pairs (Pancake, 1985). In addition, five of nineteen dyadic relationships in the subsample involved *victimization* (a repetitive pattern of physical or verbal exploitation or abuse of one child by the other; Troy and Sroufe, 1987). In each case, the *exploiter* was a child with an avoidant history, and the victim was another anxiously attached child (avoidant or resistant). Such a pattern was observed every time such a pairing occurred. Children with secure histories were never victimizers or victims. Thus, by preschool, distinctive relational patterns among children with different attachment histories clearly extend to interactions with peers.

In late middle childhood (roughly ages ten to eleven), the prospect of future intimacy is enhanced by increased capacity to form close, mutual friendships (see, for example, Bigelow, 1977; Bigelow and LaGaipa, 1975; Furman and Bierman, 1984; Selman, 1980; Selman and Schultz, 1989). The expectations of earlier periods become more elaborated by increased competencies for role-taking, communication, and understanding of how to provide nurturance and reassurance (Barnett, King, Howard, and Dino, 1980; Waters, Kondo-Ikemura, Posada, and Richters, 1991). In the Minnesota longitudinal sample, children who had been secure in their attachments at twelve to eighteen months of age were more likely to form a friendship than those who had been insecurely attached; further, they tended to form friendships with children who also had secure histories (Elicker, Englund, and Sroufe, 1992). Although this result might be attributable to a natural attraction among competent children, the qualities of these friendships also were consistent with attachment history (Shulman, Elicker, and Sroufe, 1994). The friendships of secure-secure pairs were apparent in group settings, yet the pairs also participated appropriately in group activities while maintaining their relationships with each other. In contrast, an avoidant-avoidant pair often were physically separate from others, seldom participated in voluntary groups, rarely interchanged with other individuals, and showed jealousy regarding each other. In a third pattern, resistant-resistant friends had difficulty sustaining their relationships because one of the two often was absorbed by the group, thus separating from the other. Although their relationship was not detrimental to group functioning, as avoidant-avoidant relationships were, neither was the friendship as compatible with group effectiveness as the friendships of secure children were.

Securely attached children also showed relatively more advanced mastery of social-cognitive and emotional skills that support the development of intimacy. Theoretically, experiencing secure relationships should foster empathy toward others (Elicker, Englund, and Sroufe, 1992). In the Minnesota sample, both preschool teachers' judgments of empathy and videotaped records from the classroom revealed more empathic behavior by children with secure histories than by children with anxious histories (Kestenbaum, Farber, and Sroufe, 1989; Sroufe, 1983). Moreover, children with avoidant histories, who are presumed to experience chronic rebuffs to their expressed needs, were significantly more likely than both other groups to show *anti-empathy* (behavior that would make another person's distress worse, such as taunting a crying child), whereas those with resistant histories behaved as though the distress were their own, blurring the boundary between self and other. Compared to children with histories of anxious attachment, those with histories marked by security also were more likely to incorporate people into fantasy play, to report more positive fantasized resolutions for misfortunes or interpersonal conflicts (Rosenberg, 1984), and to manifest more positive expectations regarding peers' behavior toward them (Suess, Grossmann, and Sroufe, 1993).

Members of the Minnesota sample confirm the importance of childhood relationships for the further development of capacities for intimacy during adolescence. The variations in tendencies toward positive expectations concerning peers at ages ten and eleven, described earlier, are correlated with measures of internal working models of peer relationships at ages twelve and thirteen. Furthermore, middle-childhood social competence with peers is correlated with friendship competence at age sixteen, although less so for boys than for girls (Ostoja, 1996). In general, in analyses relating data from childhood and adolescence, early history of anxious attachment is associated with problems of dependency, poor peer relationships, and lack of social understanding, and for girls, low quality of friendships in adolescence (see, for example, Ostoja, 1996; Sroufe, Carlson, and Shulman, 1993). These significant findings persist even when the characteristics of more recent relationships are statistically controlled. Thus, similar behavioral, cognitive, and affective components of relationships have been observed across the transition from middle childhood to adolescence, and this continuity may extend to intimate relationships with romantic partners.

The impressive continuities in relationships just outlined may occur for a variety of reasons. The transactional view proposed earlier in the chapter is consistent with repeated findings that both early and ongoing experience influence behavior and development. Current family functioning adds unique variance in predicting outcomes. Changing family circumstances (especially changing relationship support and maternal depression) account for change between ages. These continuities are consistent with the hypothesis that representations of relationships may account for similarity across dyads and across time. The findings also challenge researchers to investigate the possibility of further, long-term links between childhood relationships and later ones, including romantic relationships, and to provide compelling explanations for such links.

Middle-Childhood Precursors of Later Romantic Relationships

In the Minnesota Longitudinal Project, addressing this challenge began with the hypothesis that competence in romantic relationships during adolescence reflects a base of general social competence developed in the same-sex friendships and peer-group relations of middle childhood. Assessments of these competences took place in intensive observations of a subsample of participants from the longitudinal sample in summer camp programs at ages ten and eleven, and five years later in reunions of camp participants. In addition, one year following the reunions, when the participants were sixteen years old, all completed an extensive battery of measures given to the entire longitudinal sample. Part of the battery was an interview about romantic relationships and related behaviors. The procedures followed and the measures taken at each age were as follows.

Summer Camps at Ages Ten and Eleven. Forty-eight children were selected from the entire sample to participate in one-month summer day camps. These children were divided into three groups of sixteen. Each group was assigned to one of three summer camps held between 1986 and 1988. Campers were selected according to age (M = 10 years, 11 months; SD = 7 months), attachment history, gender, and race. (For full details, see Sroufe, Englund, and Urban, 1991). One boy left the last camp after five days, leaving forty-seven subjects for this first phase of the study.

The camps were held on the University of Minnesota campus. Four to five advanced graduate students and one to two advanced undergraduates served as camp counselors. All counselors had previous experience working with grade school children. The children attended for four weeks, five days a week, four and a half hours a day. They were transported to and from their homes by car or van. Activities included swimming, crafts, sports, and an overnight camp-out. Participants were videotaped whenever possible. In addition, interactions with peers were observed according to a preset daily random ordering of all participants. Observers watched a target child until one of the several codes could be assigned, before moving on to the next child to be observed. The following three measures from the camps were included in the analyses to be reported here:

1. A *friendship score* was derived from several types of social behavior coded by observers: frequency of coordinated interactions with a specific other child (such as turn-taking, sharing of objects, eye contact, and touching), and duration of these interactions. Each camper received a score calculated by combining these data for each pair in the camp. The highest interaction score for a single partner in dyads and with a partner in groups was then divided by the total number of times the target child was observed, yielding a proportional score of total observations of each child (for further details, see Sroufe, Englund, and Urban, 1991). Observer agreements for the two camps were 82.7 percent and 87.3 percent, respectively.

2. Ratings of *gender boundary behavior,* or degree of adherence to middle-childhood peer-group norms that favor interaction with same-gender peers, were the second score. Mastery of the rules and rituals of gender boundary behavior serves several important developmental functions. Maintaining boundaries provides practice in the management of arousal and impulse control and prevents premature efforts at intimacy with the opposite gender, although normative mechanisms exist for safe, limited exposure (Thorne, 1986). Measures of gender boundary behavior were based on 138 hours of videotaped camp social behavior, edited down to seven hours using an event sampling procedure. The resulting tapes documented 438 events that clearly showed each child in proximity to the opposite sex and related child-initiated interactions. Two independent coders rated each child on both of two seven-point scales: a Gender Boundary Maintenance Scale and a Gender Boundary Violation Scale (for full descriptions, see Sroufe, Carlson, and Shulman, 1993). The Gender Boundary Maintenance Scale captures active strategies children use to avoid contact with the opposite sex (such as name calling, recruiting same-gender companions, and escaping when surrounded by opposite-gender peers). To achieve a high score, children must have used these strategies actively to remain separated from the opposite gender. The Gender Boundary Violation Scale measures ways children cross gender boundaries. Children obtained a high score if they frequently associated with the opposite gender in the absence of "cover" and/or entered contexts or areas associated with the other gender, or if they showed interest in particular members of the opposite

gender. The constellation of scores that implies the greatest competence is thus a high boundary-maintenance score and a low boundary-violation score. Across all three camps, reliabilities were .67 for boundary maintenance and .79 for boundary violation. The two scales were modestly negatively correlated ($r = -.20, p < .10$).

In the summer camps, only 10 percent of observed interactions between ten- and eleven-year-olds were with peers of the opposite gender, and these exceptions almost always involved multiple boys and multiple girls rather than a solitary boy or girl with a member of the other gender. Moreover, many of the interactions were accompanied by disavowal (what Thorne, 1986, calls *border-work*) or by a "cover" that legitimized the contact (such as boys frequently hurling insults rather than expressions of interest at the same group of girls, or interacting with a child of another gender because an adult has directed it). Sroufe and colleagues (1993) reported that during middle childhood, children who violated gender boundary rules also generally showed lower social competence and were less likely than other children to have one or more friends in the group. Longitudinally, gender boundary violation was associated with a history of anxious attachment and with earlier observed interactions with parents in which parent or child or both had shown peerlike behavior toward the other.

3. A more general measure was a rating of *general social competence*. At the conclusion of each camp, counselors rank-ordered all participants in terms of their ability to function in the group, to enter and depart a group, to be attractive to others, and to provide group leadership. These rankings were added to derive a single ranking for each child. A low score thus indicates high competence. Average interrater reliability ranged from .64 to .78 across the separate camps. This measure subsequently was found to be highly intercorrelated with other measures of positive adaptation in middle childhood, including the independently derived friendship score ($r = -.58, p < .001$) (Sroufe and others, 1991).

Camp Reunions at Age Fifteen. Five years later, forty-one of the forty-seven camp participants attended reunions of their camp groups. Average ages across the three camp reunions were 15.23 years to 15.83 years. Each reunion was held at a semirural YMCA camp near Minneapolis–Saint Paul. Reunions ran from Saturday morning until Sunday afternoon (twenty-eight hours). Participants were housed in two sleeping cabins, situated approximately twenty yards apart, one for adolescent males and the male counselors, and one for adolescent females and the female counselors. Activities (structured team-building activities, free time, and meals) were held on the campgrounds and in a nearby building. Activities were videotaped whenever possible. Counselors and observers were unaware of participants' histories, including their attachment classification and social competence in middle childhood.

The primary reunion-based measure in the present analyses was the Capacity for Vulnerability Scale. This scale consisted of counselor ratings of each participant on a seven-point scale of openness, confidence, and vulnerability during interpersonally challenging situations. The measure reflects the positive theoretical expectation that a capacity for intimacy involves an openness to emotional risks rather than an overdefensiveness or fear of being hurt. Such an orientation should be especially likely in individuals who in their early relationships developed a sense of confidence that others will respond to their expressions of tender feelings with sensitivity and respect. A particular focus for raters was behavior in opposite-sex interactions; a defensive reaction could result in participants' avoidance of such interactions. Adolescents earned a high score on the measure if they openly entered into opportunities for opposite-sex interaction rather than avoiding situations in which they might be vulnerable to rejection. Counselors' ratings were added to form a composite score of capacity for vulnerability for each participant. Average pairwise reliability for scale ratings was .65 (Sroufe, Carlson, and Shulman, 1993).

Interviews at Age Sixteen. All participants in the longitudinal study completed a large battery of tests and questionnaires at age sixteen. As part of this assessment, a trained graduate student or research assistant conducted a dating interview consisting of fourteen questions with follow-up probes. Six participants from the reunions who stated they were not dating or were only casually seeing members of the opposite sex did not complete the dating interview. Thus a total of thirty-four participants remained for whom information was available from camp, reunion, and dating interview. (For a full description of the dating interview, see Egeland and others, 1994).

Five graduate student researchers coded responses from the dating interview on four separate scales. The dating status scale was based on participants' reports of whether or not they dated or had done so in the past, and on the length of their current and past dating relationships. Coders rated participants on a five-point scale, ranging from 0 (no contact with the opposite sex) to 4 (dating someone for more than two months). Intercoder reliability was .86.

Those participants who reported having a relationship of two weeks or longer ($n = 34$) were then rated on a seven-point Disclosure Scale, which assessed the amount of emotional sharing between participant and partner. To achieve a high score, participants had to provide substantial evidence and specific examples of disclosure. Next, those participants who had been dating the same partner for two months or more ($n = 12$ males and 13 females) were rated on two additional seven-point scales. The Security Scale assessed participants' expectations that their partners would be available, considerate, and respectful of their feelings and needs. The Intimacy Scale rated degree of emotional closeness perceived in the relationship. Reliabilities were .81 (disclosure), .68 (security), and .80 (intimacy).

The sixteen-year-old assessment also included the Adolescent Health Survey (AHS), a self-report measure of risk factors for physical and/or emotional ill health (Blum, Resnick, and Bergeisen, 1989). One domain of the AHS covers sexual behavior, including whether or not the participant had engaged in sexual intercourse, age of first intercourse, number of sexual partners, and use of contraception. No participants reported homosexual encounters; consequently, this report refers only to heterosexual dating and sexual experiences.

Results

These measures provide initial information on the relation between peer competence in middle childhood and romantic relationships and related behavior at age sixteen. Schmit (1996) found that the friendship score in middle childhood was correlated significantly with security with dating partners ($r = .48$, $p < .005$). Correlations between the friendship score and dating disclosure and intimacy were marginally significant as well (r's $= .28$ for both, p's $< .10$). The friendship score, however, was negligibly correlated ($r = -.03$) with whether or not a young person is currently dating or has dated in the past.

The links between middle-childhood competence and dating in adolescence may be mediated by scores on the Capacity for Vulnerability Scale. Schmit (1996) tested the hypothesis that the friendship score and social competence in middle childhood were associated with capacity for vulnerability, which in turn predicts dating in adolescence. He found that the middle-childhood social competence rating was significantly correlated with capacity for vulnerability (Pearson $r = -.52$, $p < .001$). Moreover, measures of both friendship and gender boundary maintenance behavior in middle childhood were also associated with capacity for vulnerability at age fifteen (Pearson r's $= .38$ and .39, respectively; p's $< .005$). In turn, capacity for vulnerability, which had been measured in the reunions at age fifteen, was associated with three of the four measures from the dating interview one year later. The correlations were as follows: with dating intimacy, $r = .36$; with dating security, $r = .44$ (for both, $p < .05$); and with dating disclosure, $r = .63$ ($p < .001$). These findings provide support for meaningful continuities between middle-childhood peer relationships and adaptation to the challenges of dating in middle adolescence. Moreover, the possible mediating role of a capacity for vulnerability is a potentially valuable clue to psychosocial processes in the development of heterosexuality.

Schmit's (1996) demonstration of general continuity in interpersonal adaptations across time leaves open the question of how individual differences in middle childhood experience are manifested in specific behaviors commonly associated with romantic experience during adolescence. Attachment models of relational development imply that particular adaptations during adolescence should be more likely for individuals with certain characteristic experiences in childhood relationships. To test one set of specific predictions, Hennighausen (1996) undertook further analyses of the association between degree of adherence to gender boundary norms in middle childhood and sexual behavior during adolescence.

Hennighausen found that scores on neither the Gender Boundary Maintenance Scale nor the Gender Boundary Violation Scale correlated significantly with dating status for either females or males. However, as predicted, females who maintained gender boundaries in preadolescence had significantly higher scores on the security and disclosure scales for their adolescent dating relationships (Kendall's tau-b's $= .47$ and .37, respectively; p's $< .05$). For males, Gender Boundary Violation scores were inversely related to a tendency to disclose to later romantic partners, although the tendency was only marginally significant (Kendall's tau-b = –.26; p < .10).

Hennighausen's analyses also showed that both males and females who as preadolescents had followed gender boundary rules became sexually active at later ages (Kendall's tau-b's = .30 for Gender Boundary Maintenance scores and-.28 for Gender Boundary Violation scores; p's < .05 and .01, respectively). The correlation with Gender Boundary Maintenance was especially strong for females (Kendall's tau-b = .75; p < .001). Moreover, females who failed to maintain gender boundaries in middle childhood were less likely to use contraception frequently during sexual encounters in adolescence (Kendall's tau-b = –.49; p < .01); and females' tendencies to violate gender boundaries in middle childhood were positively associated with their infrequent use of contraception as adolescents (Kendall's tau-b = .32; p < .10). For males, tendencies to violate gender boundaries in middle childhood were associated with a greater number of sex partners by age sixteen (Kendall's tau-b = .33; p < .01).

These findings support the prediction that gender boundary maintenance is a salient developmental task of middle childhood that is implicated in greater competence in managing sexual aspects of adolescent dating relationships. As with Schmit's (1996) findings, Hennighausen's results show that meaningful links across time occur not only in the degree to which individuals engage in particular behaviors in relationships, but also in the quality of experiences associated with those behaviors.

These initial results underscore the need for further analyses of the processes linking relationship experiences before adolescence to the specific characteristics of romantic relationships in middle and late adolescence. In the Minnesota study, follow-up measures of relationships at seventeen and a half and nineteen are now being coded and analyzed. These additional data may provide further information about the specific course of romantic relationships for individuals whose experiences in relationships in earlier life periods differ in significant aspects.

Criteria for Further Developmental Research on Romantic Relationships

The findings of the Minnesota Longitudinal Project imply that several conditions could further illuminate the development of romantic relationships (Collins and Sroufe, in press): longitudinal assessments of relationships, attention to multiple types of relationships, and multiple independent assessments of each type of relationship.

Longitudinal Assessments. Research on the development of romantic relationships depends fundamentally on valid assessments of significant relationships before and during adolescence. Consequently, developmental research on romantic relationships must include multiple longitudinal assessments of parent-child relationships, peer relationships, and relationship representations. With such data one can determine whether early attachment experiences predict adult relationship qualities beyond predictions from later family experiences, how predictions from attachment measures fare in comparison to peer data, and whether both family and peer data make independent contributions. Comprehensive information also will eventually permit us to address process issues such as whether and how attachment experiences are mediated through peer relationships and whether and how relationship experiences are carried forward across phases of development.

Assessment of Multiple Types of Relationships. Assessment of both parent-adolescent and peer interactions is integral to this approach. Measures of relationships with parents should tap both characteristics of connectedness and autonomy. Grotevant and Cooper (1985) have provided widely emulated models of coding procedures to get at these qualities in laboratory-based observations of adolescents with their mothers and fathers. Using a similar conceptual framework, Allen, Hauser, Bell, and O'Connor (1994) developed codes for behaviors that encourage both autonomy and relatedness. All of these researchers have demonstrated lawful links between these relational patterns and adolescent ego development and skills that support a capacity for intimacy (such as role-taking skills and identity development). Having such measures of family relationships, in addition to early attachment assessments, should enhance predictions of intimacy.

The Minnesota Longitudinal Project has extended the concept of balance to other aspects of relationships between parents and adolescents that may be relevant to eventual functioning in romantic relationships. After observing parents and thirteen-year-olds complete tasks together, coders completed three distinct rating tasks (Sroufe, 1991). Coders first attended to balance between individuals, with particular emphasis on whether each person appeared to feel safe in taking a position and maintaining an opinion even in the face of disagreements. They next focused on the balance between individuals and relationships, similar to the Grotevant and Cooper (1985) and Allen, Hauser, Bell, and O'Connor (1994) balance between individuality and connectedness. Finally, they coded information about the balance between the relationship and the external world. Conceptually related to Reiss's (1984) work on *closure,* this balance refers to the degree to which a relationship system can maintain integrity while negotiating external demands (such as the strictures of an experimenter's instructions or the stress of the parent's workplace or the child's school). This extensive coding provides a relatively full picture of key components of intimacy in parent-adolescent relationships that may affect both the desire to engage in romantic relationships and success in doing so. These measures were found to be related not only to competence with peers in adolescence, especially capacity for vulnerability (Sroufe, Egeland, and Carlson, in press), but also to Adult Attachment Interview (AAI) assessments at age nineteen (Weinfield, Ogawa, and Sroufe, under review). Those children in relationships rated higher on a composite of the three balance scales at age thirteen were significantly more likely to be secure ("autonomous") on the AAI. Those judged to be "dismissing" (the adult category equivalent of avoidant) on the

AAI had earlier been in relationships more likely to be rated as low on engagement and conflict resolution and high on negative affectivity. This profile is the expected pattern in relationships undergirded by avoidance.

Assessing relationships with peers during adolescence requires methods that are different from both those appropriate for parents and adolescents and those that are valuable in research with peers during childhood. Hartup (1996) has advocated assessment of subjective as well as observable qualities in developmental research on the functions of peer relationships. Interviews with children and adolescents about peer relationships provide valuable information about the salience of a particular relationship to a young person, the effectiveness of the processes that comprise the interactions between the two peers, the coherence of representations of the relationship, and the degree to which the relationship contributes positively to individual growth. Although more difficult, especially among older children and adolescents, direct observations of peer interaction may yield information that is predictive of the nature and course of later romantic relationships. Observational studies have revealed differences between pairs of children and preadolescents previously identified as friends or acquaintances. These differences appear to be related partly to contrasting degrees of intimacy and felt security between partners (see, for example, Nelson and Aboud, 1985; Newcomb, Brady, and Hartup, 1979). Observations of adolescents in larger groups can yield information about aspects of functioning in the social crowds in which dating relationships are embedded (see, for example, Englund, Levy, and Hyson, 1997).

Multiple Independent Assessments of Each Relationship. Representations of relationships should be assessed independently. A central idea in attachment models of relational development is that children form expectations based on salient relationship experiences. These expectations are presumed to guide encounters with the environment and interpretations of experience (Main, Kaplan, and Cassidy, 1985; Sroufe and Fleeson, 1986). In the Minnesota Longitudinal Project, variations in representations, as assessed through play, story completions, and interview techniques, can indeed be predicted from relationship history. For example, representations of self and relationships derived from family drawings at age eight (McCrone, Egeland, Kalkoske, and Carlson, 1994), as well as from projective tests at age twelve and interviews at age sixteen (Ostoja and others, 1995; Weinfield, Ogawa, and Sroufe, under review), were related to direct measures of social competence at that time; they further showed stability across time (for example, the multiple R of the eight-year and twelve-year representational measures and the sixteen-year representational measure was .38). Finally, the representational measures are each related to experiential history as required by theory. Infant attachment history, for example, is related to each of these assessments in childhood and adolescence.

This framework for collecting data affords both the most comprehensive basis and the most promising prospect for establishing a link between early and intermediate close relationships and the emergence of romantic relationships during adolescence. Without intervening measures of experience and representation, questions of how much of the relation between infant and adult measures is direct and how much is mediated cannot be addressed, nor can questions concerning change in internal working models or the relation between changing models and changing relationship experiences. These alternative explanations must be examined if we are to understand the integral role of relationships in the emergence of romantic experiences during adolescence.

References

Ainsworth, M.D.S., Blehar, M., Waters, E., and Wall, S. *Patterns of Attachment*. Hillsdale, N.J.: Erlbaum, 1978.

Allen, J. P., Hauser, S. T., Bell, K. L., and O'Connor, T. G. "Longitudinal Assessment of Autonomy and Relatedness in Adolescent-Family Interactions as Predictors of Adolescent Ego Development and Self-Esteem." *Child Development*, 1994, *65*, 179–194.

Barnett, M., King, L., Howard, J., and Dino, G. "Empathy in Young Children: Relation to Parents' Empathy, Affection, and Emphasis on the Feelings of Others." *Developmental Psychology*, 1980, *16*, 243–244.

Bigelow, B. J. "Children's Friendship Expectations: A Cognitive-Developmental Study." *Child Development*, 1977, *48*, 246–253.

Bigelow, B. J., and LaGaipa, J. J. "Children's Written Descriptions of Friendship: A Multidimensional Analysis." *Developmental Psychology*, 1975, *11*, 857–858.

Blum, R. W., Resnick, M. D., and Bergeisen, L. G. *The State of Adolescent Health in Minnesota*. Minneapolis: University of Minnesota Adolescent Health Program, 1989.

Bowlby, J. *Separation*. New York: Basic Books, 1973.

Collins, W. A., and Sroufe, L. A. "Capacity for Intimate Relationships: A Developmental Construction." In W. Furman, C. Feiring, and B. B. Brown (eds.), *Contemporary Perspectives on Adolescent Romantic Relationships*. New York: Cambridge University Press, in press.

Egeland, B., and Brunnquell, D. "An At-Risk Approach to the Study of Child Abuse: Some Preliminary Findings." *Journal of the American Academy of Child Psychiatry*, 1979, *18*, 219–225.

Egeland, B., Lehn, L., Ostoja, E., Williams, F., and Kalkoske, M. "Dating Interview and Coding Scales." Unpublished manuscript, Institute of Child Development, University of Minnesota, 1994.

Elicker, J., Englund, M., and Sroufe, L. A. "Predicting Peer Competence and Peer Relationships in Childhood from Early Parent-Child Relationships." In R. Parke and G. Ladd (eds.), *Family-Peer Relationships: Modes of Linkage*. Hillsdale, N.J.: Erlbaum, 1992.

Englund, M., Levy, A., and Hyson, D. "Development of Adolescent Social Competence: A Prospective Study of Family and Peer Contributions." Poster presented at the biennial meeting of the Society for Research on Child Development, Washington, D.C., March 1997.

Furman, W., and Bierman, K. "Children's Conceptions of Friendship: A Multimethod Study of Developmental Changes." *Developmental Psychology*, 1984, *20*, 925–931.

Grotevant, H., and Cooper, C. "Patterns of Interaction in Family Relationships and the Development of Identity Exploration in Adolescence." *Child Development*, 1985, *56*, 415–428.

Hartup, W. W. "The Company They Keep: Friendships and Their Developmental Significance." *Child Development*, 1996, *67*, 1–13.

Hennighausen, K. C. "Connecting Preadolescent Gender Boundary Behavior to Adolescent Dating and Sexual Activity." Unpublished manuscript, Institute of Child Development, University of Minnesota, Minneapolis, 1996.

Hinde, R. A., and Stevenson-Hinde, J. "Interpersonal Relationships and Child Development." *Developmental Review*, 1987, *7*, 1–21.

Katchadourian, H. "Sexuality." In S. S. Feldman and G. R. Elliott (eds.), *At the Threshold: The Developing Adolescent*. Cambridge, Mass.: Harvard University Press, 1990.

Kestenbaum, R., Farber, E., and Sroufe, L. A. "Individual Differences in Empathy Among Preschoolers: Relation to Attachment History." In N. Eisenberg (ed.), *Empathy and Related Emotional Responses*. San Francisco: Jossey-Bass, 1989.

Liberman, A. F. "Preschoolers' Competence with a Peer: Relations with Attachment and Peer Experience." *Child Development*, 1977, *48*, 1277–1287.

Main, M., Kaplan, N., and Cassidy, J. "Security in Infancy, Childhood, and Adulthood: A Move to the Level of Representation." In I. Bretherton and E. Waters (eds.), *Growing Points in Attachment Theory and Research*. Monographs of the Society for Research in Child Development, no. 50 (Whole no. 209), 1985.

McCrone, E. R., Egeland, B., Kalkoske, M., and Carlson, E. "Relations Between Early Maltreatment and Mental Representations of Relationships Assessed with Projective Storytelling in Middle Childhood." *Development and Psychopathology*, 1994, *6*, 99–120.

Nelson, J., and Aboud, F. E. "The Resolution of Social Conflict Between Friends." *Child Development*, 1985, *56*, 1009–1017.

Newcomb, A. F., Brady, J., and Hartup, W. W. "Friendship and Incentive Condition as Determinants of Children's Task-Oriented Social Behavior." *Child Development*, 1979, *50*, 878–881.

Ostoja, E. "Developmental Antecedents of Friendship Competence in Adolescence: The Roles of Early Adaptational History and Middle Childhood Peer Competence." Unpublished doctoral dissertation, University of Minnesota, 1996.

Ostoja, E., McCrone, E., Lehn, L., Reed, T., and Sroufe, L. A. "Representations of Close Relationships in Adolescence: Longitudinal Antecedents from Infancy Through Childhood." Paper presented at the biennial meeting of the Society for Research in Child Development, March 1995.

Pancake, V. R. "Continuity Between Mother-Infant Attachment and Ongoing Dyadic Peer Relationships in Preschool." Paper presented at the biennial meeting of the Society for Research in Child Development, Toronto, April 1985.

Reis, H. T., and Shaver, P. "Intimacy as an Interpersonal Process." In S. W. Duck (ed.), *Handbook of Personal Relationships*. New York: Wiley, 1988.

Reiss, D. *The Family's Construction of Reality*. Cambridge, Mass.: Harvard University Press, 1984.

Rosenberg, D. M. "The Quality and Content of Preschool Fantasy Play: Correlates in Concurrent Social-Personality Function and Early Mother-Child Attachment Relationships." Unpublished doctoral dissertation, University of Minnesota, 1984.

Savin-Williams, R. C. *"And Then I Became Gay": Stories from the Lives of Gay and Bisexual Youths*. London: Routledge, in press.

Schmit, D. T. "Continuity and Change in Heterosexual Relations from Middle Childhood to Adolescence: Evidence from a Longitudinal Study." Unpublished manuscript, Department of Psychology, College of St. Catherine, Minneapolis, Minnesota, 1996.

Selman, R. L. *The Growth of Interpersonal Understanding*. Orlando: Academic Press, 1980.

Selman, R. L., and Schultz, L. H. "Children's Strategies for Interpersonal Negotiation with Peers: An Interpretive/Empirical Approach to the Study of Social Development." In T. J. Berndt and G. W. Ladd (eds.), *Peer Relationships in Child Development*. New York: Wiley, 1989.

Shulman, S., Elicker, J., and Sroufe, L. A. "Stages of Friendship Growth in Preadolescence as Related to Attachment History." *Journal of Social and Personal Relationships*, 1994, *11*, 341–361.

Sroufe, J. "Assessment of Parent-Adolescent Relationships: Implications for Adolescent Development." *Journal of Family Psychology*, 1991, *5* (1), 21–45.

Sroufe, L. A. "Infant-Caregiver Attachment and Patterns of Adaptation in Preschool: The Roots of Maladaptation and Competence." In M. Perlmutter (ed.), *Minnesota Symposium in Child Psychology*, Vol. 16. Hillsdale, N.J.: Erlbaum, 1983.

Sroufe, L. A. "Pathways to Adaptation and Maladaptation: Psychopathology as Developmental Deviation." In D. Cicchetti (ed.), *Rochester Symposia on Developmental Psychopathology,* Vol. 1. Hillsdale, N.J.: Erlbaum, 1989.

Sroufe, L. A., Bennett, C., Englund, M., Urban, J., and Shulman, S. "The Significance of Gender Boundaries in Preadolescence: Contemporary Correlates and Antecedents of Boundary Violation and Maintenance." *Child Development,* 1993, *64* (2), 455–466.

Sroufe, L. A., Carlson, E., and Shulman, S. "The Development of Individuals in Relationships: From Infancy Through Adolescence." In D. C. Funder, R. Parke, C. Tomlinson-Keasey, and K. Widaman (eds.), *Studying Lives Through Time: Approaches to Personality and Development.* Washington D.C.: American Psychological Association, 1993.

Sroufe, L. A., Egeland, B., and Carlson, E. "One Social World." In W. A. Collins and B. Laursen (eds.), *Relationships as Developmental Contexts: The Minnesota Symposia on Child Psychology,* Vol. 30. Hillsdale, N.J.: Erlbaum, in press.

Sroufe, L. A., Englund, M., and Urban, J. "Camp Manual." Unpublished manuscript, University of Minnesota, Minneapolis, 1991.

Sroufe, L. A., and Fleeson, J. "Attachment and the Construction of Relationships." In W. W. Hartup and Z. Rubin (eds.), *Relationships and Development.* Hillsdale, N.J.: Erlbaum, 1986.

Suess, G. J., Grossmann, K. E., and Sroufe, L. A. "Effects of Infant Attachment to Mother and Father on Quality of Adaptation in Preschool: From Dyadic to Individual Organization of Self." *International Journal of Behavioral Development,* 1993, *15* (1), 43–66.

Sullivan, H. S. *The Interpersonal Theory of Psychiatry.* New York: Norton, 1953.

Thorne, B. "Girls and Boys Together . . . But Mostly Apart: Gender Arrangements in Elementary Schools." In W. W. Hartup and Z. Rubin (eds.), *Relationships and Development.* Hillsdale, N.J.: Erlbaum, 1986.

Troy, M., and Sroufe, L. A. "Victimization Among Preschoolers: The Role of Attachment Relationship History." *Journal of the American Academy of Child and Adolescent Psychiatry,* 1987, *26* (2), 166–172.

Waters, E., Kondo-Ikemura, K., Posada, G., and Richters, J. E. "Learning to Love: Mechanisms and Milestones." In M. Gunnar and L. A. Sroufe (eds.), *Minnesota Symposia on Child Psychology,* Vol. 23: *Self Processes and Development.* Hillsdale, N.J.: Erlbaum, 1991.

Waters, E., and Sroufe, L. A. "Social Competence as a Developmental Construct." *Developmental Review,* 1983, *3,* 79–97.

Weinfield, N., Ogawa, J., and Sroufe, L. A. "Early Attachment as a Pathway to Adolescent Peer Competence." Under review.

Zani, B. "Dating and Interpersonal Relationship in Adolescence." In S. Jackson and H. Rodriguez-Tome (eds.), *Adolescence and Its Social Worlds.* Hillsdale, N.J.: Erlbaum, 1993.

Zeanah, C. H., and Zeanah, P. D. "Intergenerational Transmission of Maltreatment: Insights from Attachment Theory and Research." *Psychiatry,* 1989, *52,* 177–196.

W. ANDREW COLLINS *is professor at the Institute of Child Development, University of Minnesota.*

KATHERINE C. HENNIGHAUSEN *is a doctoral student at the Institute of Child Development, University of Minnesota.*

DAVID TAYLOR SCHMIT *is associate professor of psychology at the College of St. Catherine, Minneapolis, Minnesota.*

L. ALAN SROUFE *is professor at the Institute of Child Development, University of Minnesota.*

Same-gender and cross-gender friendships are examined as potential contexts for the development of social preferences and skills that may influence the quality of adolescent dating relationships and adult marriages.

Gender Development and Heterosexual Romantic Relationships During Adolescence

Campbell Leaper, Kristin J. Anderson

One of the hallmarks of adolescence is the beginning of romantic relationships. Although many adolescents may either delay heterosexual dating until later years or indicate a preference for same-gender sexual partners, most will begin heterosexual relationships. The way in which adolescent girls and boys begin to relate with one another is apt to be influenced by their experiences in other types of relationships. As Furman and Wehner (1994, p. 182) recently argued, "adolescents are likely to be predisposed to respond to romantic partners as they have in other relationships." Moreover, how young women and men relate to one another in their first romantic relationships may lay the foundation for later sexual and nonsexual cross-gender relationships.[1] Despite the potentially important links between adolescents' romantic relationships and other relationships, surprisingly few comparisons have been made of these different types of relationships (Furman, 1993, p. 94). In an attempt to contribute to our thinking on this topic and possibly stimulate new research directions, this chapter explores ways in which same-and cross-gender friendships may influence the quality of adolescents' and young adults' heterosexual romantic relationships. We also consider how traditional gender development may undermine the emergence of qualities associated with high degrees of satisfaction in romantic relationships.

The chapter is divided into four sections. First, we consider some of the practical reasons why it is important to examine adolescent romantic relationships. Second, we consider how children's traditionally gender-segregated peer relationships contribute to miscommunications and power asymmetries in later heterosexual relationships, which in turn may lead to relationship dissatisfaction. Third, we review some of the correlates of relationship satisfaction and dysfunction in heterosexual romantic relationships. Finally, we consider possible ways to foster in adolescents the social orientations and skills associated with satisfaction in romantic relationships. Given the absence of relevant research directly testing for the links between adolescent gender development and romantic relationships, our chapter typically relies on indirect evidence to support our ideas.

Why Study Factors Related to Adolescent Romantic Relationships?

Teenage Pregnancy, Sexually Transmitted Diseases, and Dating Violence in Adolescent Heterosexual Relationships. Social scientists and laypersons alike are sounding alarms about the current state of adolescent heterosexual relationships in the United States. First, there is much concern about the widespread prevalence of teenage pregnancy (Hansen, Christopher, and Nangle, 1992; National Center for Health Statistics, 1993). Nearly two-fifths of adolescent girls become pregnant before the age of twenty. The babies born to these mothers account for nearly 13 percent of all U.S. births. The rates for teenage pregnancy and birth in the United States exceed those for any other developed country. These statistics are a serious cause for concern due to the great difficulties typically faced by teenage mothers and their babies. Infants born to teenage mothers are at significantly greater risk for a variety of health problems, including complications from premature birth. Most teenage mothers are single parents and one-third of them drop out of school. Lacking adequate job skills, child care, or support from the father, teenage mothers are likely to become financially dependent on either their families or welfare. In the United States, 60 percent of all women receiving Aid to Families with Dependent Children are teen mothers. In addition to being poor, teenage mothers usually do not have the social supports or parenting skills to provide adequate child rearing for their children.

A second crisis associated with adolescent heterosexual relationships is the epidemic of sexually transmitted diseases (STDs). Teenagers have the highest rate of STDs of any age group in the United States. Approximately one-fourth of adolescents contract an STD by the age of twenty-one (Department of Health and Human Services, 1996). Most important, however, is the fact that HIV infection is increasing at the fastest rate among adolescents; one-fourth of new infections in the United States occurs in teenagers.

Finally, the widespread incidence of dating violence is a serious cause for concern. Due to different definitions of what constitutes dating violence (ranging from assault to battery to rape), the rates of incidence vary somewhat across surveys. The estimates generally range between one-tenth to one-third of U.S. high school and college students have experienced physical violence in dating relationships (Bergman, 1992; Carlson, 1987; Levy, 1990). Moreover, some surveys targeting specific schools or geographic regions have reported incidences of dating violence exceeding 50 percent (Jezl, 1996; O'Keeffe, Brock-opp, and Chew, 1986).

For many teens and young adults, violence may be accepted as a normal and expected part of a dating relationship. Researchers have found, for example, that dating violence usually is not viewed by teenagers as a cause for terminating the relationship, that it is likely to recur during the course of the relationship, and that it usually may not even be recognized as violence by either partner (Bergman, 1992; Laner, 1990). Furthermore, the effects of these experiences may continue later in life. Those teenagers who experience dating violence are more likely to be victims or perpetrators of violence in their adult relationships (White and Humphrey, 1994). In addition to the impact of relationship violence on the individuals involved, the criminal costs of arresting, prosecuting, and incarcerating batterers further burdens society as a whole.

Relationship Dissatisfaction and Violence in Adult Marriages. The status of contemporary American heterosexual marriages provides additional reasons for looking back to adolescence to identify possible precursors and explore potential preventative interventions. Two issues are highlighted.

First, relationship dissatisfaction and divorce are common occurrences in most contemporary marriages in America. Approximately half of all marriages end in divorce. Although marriage is positively correlated with psychological adjustment in both women and men, the correlation is stronger for men than for women (Gove, Style, and Hughes, 1990; Wood, Rhodes, and Whelan, 1989). Also, women are twice as likely as men to initiate a divorce (National Center for Health Statistics, 1989). Therefore, women may be more likely than men not to be satisfied within the marriage, which leads to a greater likelihood to initiate divorce. After divorce, however, men are at a significantly greater risk for psychological adjustment problems (including depression and suicide) than women (McKenry and Price, 1990). Thus, the nature of marital dissatisfaction and dissolution appears somewhat different for women and men: women may be more likely to experience greater dissatisfaction inside a marriage, but men may be more apt to experience greater distress following divorce. Ultimately, both women and men suffer when marital relationships do not work.

One of the reasons for many American women's dissatisfaction in marriage and eventual divorce is domestic violence. Although men as well as women are victims of relationship violence, women are approximately ten times more likely than men to be victims of violence by an intimate partner (Bachman and Pillemer, 1992). In the United States, conservative estimates are that 10 percent of women in marriages experience physical battering, verbal abuse, or forced sex (Bagarozzi and Giddings, 1983; Bograd, 1986). Domestic violence is the leading cause of injury in the United States for women between fifteen and forty-four years of age (Federal Bureau of Investigation, 1991).

The impact of domestic violence is far-reaching and extends to any children present in the family. Over three million children are exposed to parental violence each year (Carlson, 1991), and child abuse is fifteen times more likely in families with domestic violence (Carter, Stacey, and Shupe, 1988). These experiences appear to have long-lasting effects on many of these children. Men who witnessed their parents' domestic violence when growing up are three times more likely than sons of nonviolent parents to abuse their own wives (Straus and Gelles, 1988). Conversely, women who witnessed domestic violence as children are at greater risk for entering abusive relationships (Follingstad, Rutledge, McNeill-Harkins, and Polek, 1992; Reuterman and Burcky, 1989; White and Humphrey, 1994). In these ways, the cycle of violence is repeated.

In summary, there is no shortage of sad statistics that underscore the crises occurring in women's and men's relationships: teenage pregnancy, life-threatening STDs, domestic violence, and generally unhappy lives. The risks are real for young women and men as well as for any children that result from their union. In the rest of the chapter we attempt to understand the nature of some of the problems underlying these crises. We explore some relevant factors in the development of heterosocial relationships, as well as consider some possible alternative pathways and means of intervention for improving these relationships. Some critics suggest that returning to more traditional gender roles is what is needed to solve these social problems (for example, Murray, 1995). We disagree. Instead, we argue that fostering greater gender *equality* can help to alleviate some of these current dilemmas.

In the next section we review possible origins of the emergence of traditional patterns in girls' and boys' social relationships that may contribute to later difficulties in heterosocial interactions and relationships. The maintenance of gender-segregated peer associations during childhood is targeted in particular. Afterwards, in the third part of the chapter, we consider factors related to satisfying romantic relationships. Finally, we explore how cross-gender intimacy may be fostered during development.

The Legacies of Childhood Gender Segregation in Adolescence and Adulthood

Children typically begin demonstrating preferences for same-gender peers—known as gender segregation—around the age of three. These preferences are maintained throughout childhood until heterosocial and heterosexual relationships begin to emerge during adolescence (Maccoby, 1990). Gender-differentiated developmental pathways in peer play and relationships foster corresponding gender differences in social norms and social skills (see Leaper, 1994). For instance, girls' traditional play with dolls and kitchen sets provides them with relatively more opportunities than boys to practice the social-relational skills that are typically beneficial in the private world of intimate relationships. In contrast, boys' traditional play with construction toys or in team sports gives them relatively more opportunities to practice the instrumental-assertive skills that are advantageous in the public world of work. These divergent developmental pathways are maintained by parents (Fagot, 1995; Leaper,

Anderson, and Sanders, 1997), teachers (Leaper, 1995; Lockheed, 1985; Sadker and Sadker, 1994), and peers (Leaper, 1994; Leaper and Holliday, 1995; Maccoby, 1990, 1994). Thus, by the time they reach adolescence, boys traditionally have been prepared to approach relationships more in terms of greater independence and dominance, whereas girls traditionally have been socialized to approach relationships more in terms of nurturance and support (see Leaper, 1994). Consequently, men may demonstrate a more domineering and autonomous communication style, whereas women may demonstrate a more accommodating and engaging communication style. It is our thesis that differences in social norms and social-cognitive skills resulting from children's gender-segregated peer affiliations contribute in part to later communication difficulties and power asymmetries in heterosexual romantic relationships (see Gottman and Carrere, 1994; Leaper, 1994).

The traditional masculine gender-role pathway is of particular importance for understanding the unfortunate incidence of male violence in adolescent and adult romantic relationships. Toward this end, several authors have highlighted ways that the normative experiences and rewards associated with most boys' childhoods actually potentiates the likelihood of men's violence toward women. First, at early ages, boys learn to avoid anything considered "feminine"—which typically includes social sensitivity, nurturance, and emotional expressiveness (Levant, 1995). Also, boys receive more encouragement to confront others directly (and sometimes aggressively) with their anger (Levant, 1995). For example, fistfights on the playground or in the neighborhood are common occurrences during a boy's development but are relatively rare in a girl's experience. In contrast, researchers find that girls are more likely to express their anger and aggression in less overtly aggressive ways through, for example, creating coalitions with other children (Bjorkqvist, Osterman, and Kaukiainen, 1992; Crick and Grotpeter, 1995).

Gender differences in athletic participation are also tied to corresponding differences in aggression. Although their participation in sports such as baseball, basketball, track, and soccer has increased during recent years, girls rarely engage in highly aggressive contact sports such as football, hockey, and boxing. Journalists and social scientists have noted that these contact sports are sanctioned contexts in which it is acceptable for boys and men to act in physically aggressive ways (Messner and Sabo, 1994; Miedzian, 1991; Nelson, 1994). Moreover, the emphasis on physical aggression in these sports has been correlated with positive attitudes toward sexism and male dominance as well as higher incidences of violence toward women (see Messner and Sabo, 1994). For example, Koss and Dinero (1988) found that college athletes are responsible for approximately one-third of reported campus sexual assaults. Thus the culture of violence that predominates in many boys' world of sports may orient some men toward violence in close relationships (see Messner and Sabo, 1994; Nelson, 1994).

There is some evidence that tolerance for male aggression may have unfortunate consequences on later romantic relationships. Several researchers have reported a greater likelihood of dating violence among adolescent boys and girls who were more accepting toward male dominance and aggression (Follingstad, Rutledge, McNeill-Harkins, and Polek, 1992; Hansen, Christopher, and Nangle, 1992; Lundberg-Love and Geffner, 1989; White and Humphrey, 1994; White and Koss, 1993). The findings are only correlational, however, and it is unclear to what extent tolerant attitudes regarding male aggression actually contribute to the likelihood that some boys will act violently or that some girls will enter into abusive relationships. Additional developmental research is needed to test the link between children's and adolescents' participation in aggressive sports, tolerance for aggression, and later functioning in romantic relationships.

We have reviewed some of the traditional ways in which many boys are engaged in social contexts that value dominance and overt aggression. Turning to girls, we can also note ways that they are usually involved in social situations stressing interpersonal sensitivity and closeness. Accordingly, we know from various studies that girls are generally more likely than boys to develop intimate friendships during adolescence. Whereas most adolescent girls appear to establish intimate friendships characterized by reciprocal disclosures and mutual support, adolescent boys are much more variable (Berndt, 1992; Buhrmester and Furman, 1987; Camarena, Sarigiani, and Petersen; 1990; Sharabany, Gershoni, and Hofman, 1981). For example, when Youniss and Smollar (1985) examined same-gender friendship qualities in adolescents, they found that two-thirds of adolescent girls had close friendships characterized by mutual openness and intimacy, but fewer than half of adolescent boys had similarly close same-gender friendships. Relatedly, when asked to indicate a problem in their friendships, adolescent boys were more likely than girls to mention a lack of reciprocation or help (approximately 25 percent versus 7 percent, respectively). Thus, given the emphasis on emotional control and competition associated with boys' childhood peer groups, establishing friendship intimacy may pose a greater challenge to boys than to girls. Furthermore, to the extent that they have viewed same-gender friendship intimacy differently, many adolescent boys and girls may also enter romantic relationships with different perspectives. For instance, when Feiring (1995) asked fifteen-year-old adolescents to evaluate various qualities in romantic relationships, more than half of the girls but only one-third of the boys mentioned intimacy as an advantage (54 percent versus 32 percent, respectively).

In sum, research strongly suggests that from an early age girls' and boys' gender-segregated and gender-normed peer relationships tend to provide different experiences and promote different skills, which may clash later when young women and men come together to form heterosexual romantic relationships. Now that we have considered some of the developmental processes that may possibly foster later difficulties and problems in heterosexual romantic relationships, we next examine some of the factors related to *satisfying* romantic relationships.

What Accounts for Satisfying Romantic Relationships?

During recent decades there has been an increasing trend toward greater gender equality in sexual and work relationships in the United States and other western societies. Despite these changes, most heterosexual dating relationships still tend to follow traditional roles. For example, in a recent survey of 413 heterosexually dating undergraduates, Felmlee (1994) found that fewer than half perceived their relationships to be equal in the distribution of power. Imbalances in decision making, emotional involvement, and overall equity were most commonly reported. Men were twice as likely as women to be viewed as the one with more power. Conversely, women were seen as more emotionally engaged in the relationship. These differences reflect the traditional model of heterosexual relationships described by Parsons and Bales (1955) in which the husband takes on the role of "instrumental leader" while the wife assumes the role of "socioemotional leader."

Although change may be slow, there is evidence to support the trend toward equality in love relationships. Egalitarian relationships are generally associated with high degrees of satisfaction in studies of heterosexual romantic relationships (Blumstein and Schwartz, 1983; Hecht, Marston, and Larkey, 1994; Kurdek and Schmitt, 1986; Winn, Crawford, and Fischer, 1991) and homosexual romantic relationships (Blumstein and Schwartz, 1983; Kurdek and Schmitt, 1986), as well as same-gender friendships (Winn, Crawford, and Fischer, 1991).

If egalitarian relationships are not based on a complementarity of roles, as proposed in Parsons and Bales's model, then how is equality expressed in these relationships? To a large extent, both the woman and the man share the roles as socioemotional and instrumental leaders. Thus there is a combination of mutual decision making (instrumental function) and mutual expressiveness and support (socioemotional function). Relationship equality defined in this way is largely accomplished through communication. Accordingly, the research literature strongly indicates that friends as well as dating couples who have similar communication skills are more likely to have mutually satisfying, long-lasting relationships (see Burleson and Samter, 1994). However, as described earlier in the chapter, traditional gender development tends to foster different communication styles in girls and boys. Indeed, when surveyed about the kinds of dating problems they most often encounter, a sample of 334 college students often mentioned difficulties in communication (Knox and Wilson, 1983). For women, frequently cited problems included "unwanted pressure to engage in sexual behavior" (23 percent), "sexual misunderstandings" (9 percent), and "communication with date" (20 percent). For men, the most commonly mentioned problems included "communication with date" (35 percent) and "honesty/openness" (8 percent). Thus, both women and men often noted difficulties communicating and relating with one another. For the women, there were additional complaints about negotiating sexual boundaries. The situation does not seem to change in marriage. Marriage counselors are regularly confronted with couples having difficulties communicating with each other (Gottman, 1994). The pervasiveness of communication difficulties in contemporary heterosexual relationships is also reflected by the seemingly endless appearance of best-selling books on love relationships and communication.

If many teenage girls and boys as well as adult women and men are having problems talking and relating with one another, what aspects of communication are tied to satisfying love relationships? Two sets of processes have been emphasized in the research literature: self-disclosure and listener support, and disagreement and conflict.

Mutual Self-Disclosure. Self-disclosure is an effective strategy for expressing and freeing one's feelings, revealing and sharing one's self with a partner, as well as allowing for the opportunity to get some validation and insight from the partner's feedback. Therefore, it should be no surprise that studies generally show a strong correlation between mutual self-disclosure and married couples' relationship satisfaction (Hendrick, 1981). The same appears true in adolescent romantic relationships as well. Hansen, Christopher, and Nangle (1992) reviewed various conversational skills correlated with successful heterosocial interactions and relationships, and self-disclosure and listener support were the most important predictors.

Traditional gender differences in expressiveness may contribute to frustrations in heterosexual relationships. There is a tendency toward less self-disclosure in boys' and men's friendships than in girls' and women's friendships (Dindia and Allen, 1992; Hill and Stull, 1987). However, studies suggest that the difference may be in preference rather than ability. Adolescent boys and young men appear willing to disclose to female friends but not to male friends (Reisman, 1990; Youniss and Smollar, 1985).

The influence of the partner's gender on boys' and men's willingness to self-disclose reflects the fact that gender differences in intimacy are partly a function of self-presentational concerns (Deaux and Major, 1987). Researchers have interpreted this situational variation as reflecting boys' and men's concern with appearing masculine with their male friends (see Leaper, 1994). However, to the extent that adolescent boys spend most of their time with male friends, these self-presentational concerns may limit the kinds of social skills they exercise and develop. If adolescent boys and young men avoid disclosing with one another, they will also be avoiding opportunities to refine the social skills associated with being a supportive listener. Thus, a difference in preference may develop into a difference in ability.

Besides sharing one's feelings, a reciprocal component of an intimate relationship is being a good listener. In their review of various conversational skills associated with satisfying heterosocial relationships, Hansen, Christopher, and Nangle (1992) indicated that acknowledging the other and showing support were related to successful interactions. Conversely, making negative statements and being nonresponsive to the other's statements were associated with heterosocial difficulties. Thus, in addition to sharing one's thoughts and feelings, it is necessary to know how to be a good listener. In many romantic relationships, however, it appears that the man may receive his romantic partner's support but not reciprocate that support in response to her disclosures (Tannen, 1990).

An example of how gender differences in listener support may tend to occur was suggested in a recent study looking at young adults' conversations with a friend. Leaper and colleagues (1995) studied eighteen- to twenty-two-year-olds discussing their family relationships with either a same-gender or cross-gender friend. The listener's verbal responses following the friend's self-disclosure were analyzed in terms of levels of support and responsiveness. Some of the coded listening responses included active understanding (reflective, supportive statements), back channel listening statements (for example, "um-hmm"), and abstaining responses (no verbal response following a self-disclosure). Active understanding listener responses to friends' self-disclosures occurred proportionally more for women with female friends (27 percent) than for either women with male friends (13 percent), men with male friends (14 percent), or men with female friends (14 percent). The implication for heterosexual relationships is that many women may find themselves unsatisfied with the man's degree of listener support. The man, however, may be enjoying the rewards of the woman's responsiveness.

The interaction between individual and situational factors is emphasized in Deaux and Major's (1987) theoretical model of gender. Individual cognitive factors include the person's self-presentational concerns, attitudes, and social schemas, and situational factors include aspects of the interactive setting such as the activity and the gender of the participants. Correlational studies suggest a relationship between gender schemas and expressiveness in romantic relationships. For example, relationship quality and relationship satisfaction were higher among couples in which both partners have either "feminine" (socioemotional) or "androgynous" (combined instrumental and socioemotional) self-concepts (Kurdek and Schmitt, 1986). Also, individuals with "androgynous" self-concepts reported greater willingness to self-disclose than those with traditional gender self-concepts (Sollie and Fischer, 1985).

The previously cited evidence linking gender attitudes and schemas to relationship qualities is limited to correlational studies. Therefore, it is difficult to discern the extent to which people's attitudes direct versus reflect their behavior. Some experimental studies have highlighted how situational factors may be causally related to gender variations in individuals' behavior. For example, research was cited earlier indicating that men were more likely to self-disclose with women than with men friends. In addition to the friend's gender, the activity setting is another factor that may contribute to one's willingness to self-disclose. Several studies have shown that women and men tend to differ in their topic preferences during conversation (see Bischoping, 1993). Specifically, women were more apt to talk about other people, whereas men were more apt to talk about things they do (for example, sports, work). However, when studies have assigned particular topics to discuss, an interesting finding emerges: the conversation topic rather than the speaker's (or the listener's) gender accounts for much of the variation in communication style. For example, in our own research (Anderson and Leaper, 1997), we asked young women and men to discuss different topics with one of their friends. In a self-disclosure situation, they were asked to discuss how their family relations have changed since entering college. In an unstructured situation, we allowed them to discuss whatever they wanted. When we analyzed the participants' conversational content for emotional expression, conversational topic was more predictive of emotion expression than was gender. In particular, we found relatively few references to negative emotions for either women or men in the unstructured setting compared to the self-disclosure topic. Furthermore, when negative emotions were discussed during the self-disclosure topic, speakers were more likely to refer to negative emotions using indirect phrases rather than explicit emotion terms. Thus, the assigned topic predicted the type of emotion discussed (positive or negative) as well as the linguistic form (direct or indirect) that was used to express emotions.

Conflict and Disagreement. Research indicates that another important predictor of relationship satisfaction and adjustment is the couple's capacity to engage in conversations about their disagreements (Gottman, 1993; Kurdek and Schmitt, 1986). Moreover, relationship satisfaction is strongly tied to the ability of one partner to bring up disagreements without the other partner either withdrawing or countercomplaining (Gottman, 1993). For example, withdrawal by husbands during discussions of issues initiated by the wife can reliably predict a decline in wives' relationship satisfaction (Heavey, Christensen, and Malamuth, 1995). Men's withdrawal during conflict with their partners may be a result of men's fear of relationship connectedness (Bergman, 1995). Also, there is some evidence suggesting that men tend to have more difficulty than women regulating negative affect during interpersonal conflicts. In support of this argument, Gottman and Levenson (1988) observed higher levels of autonomic arousal among husbands than wives during a marital conflict. One possible reaction is a "flight" response in the form of withdrawal and avoidance (Gottman, 1993; Heavey, Christensen, and Malamuth, 1995). However, an alternative reaction can be a "fight" response in the form of lashing out through physical abuse (Babcock, Waltz, Jacobson, and Gottman, 1993). Additionally, as Noller (1993) postulates, men's silence during relationship conflicts may function to maintain their power over the situation. The person who withdraws leaves the other person powerless to resolve the conflict.

The correlations between men's withdrawal and emotional arousal during conflict does not establish the causal relationship (if any) between these factors. Some of the relevant research questions for developmental investigators to consider include the following: Are some men less communicative about their feelings during conflict resulting from their heightened levels of arousal? Or do these men experience heightened arousal during conflicts because they are not used to discussing their feelings? Or does avoiding emotion-laden material become a vicious cycle in boys' and men's lives? We consider some possible answers.

Because boys and men attempt to control their emotions, they may become more aroused when confronted with interpersonal conflicts. When with their male friends, boys and men can intentionally avoid emotion-laden topics. Recall that studies indicate that men are less likely to discuss personal matters with their men friends (Bischoping, 1993). To the extent that people are more at ease in familiar than in unfamiliar situations, it may be that men who grew up learning to hide their feelings are at risk for relatively heightened autonomic arousal when their wives bring up emotional topics. For these men, verbal intimacy may be an unfamiliar context in which they perceive themselves having little control. This interpretation may also explain the common complaint among women that men respond to their self-disclosures with advice (for example, Tannen, 1990). Advising a solution is a way to restore a sense of control and get the issue out of the way. This gender difference seems to appear in gay and lesbian relationships as well. Kurdek and Schmitt (1986) found evidence that men in gay romantic relationships were more likely than women in lesbian relationships to report difficulties in communicating about inner thoughts and feelings (expectations for "mind reading").

According to some researchers (Bergman, 1995; Miller, Danaher, and Forbes, 1986; Tannen, 1990), girls (and women) differ from boys (and men) in how they view and respond to conflict. For the traditional man, disagreements may be interpreted as *competition* for viewpoints. In contrast, for the traditional woman, disagreements may be interpreted more as opportunities to *share* perspectives (Bergman, 1995). Paradoxically, each party may find the other's approach confrontive. The traditional woman may find the man's competition-for-viewpoints approach as domineering and insensitive, whereas the traditional man may find the woman's expectation for reciprocal disclosure as threatening to his sense of control. Consequently, miscommunication would occur between the partners. However, the outcome affects the woman and the man asymmetrically because it favors the man's control and dominance over the relationship (Henley, 1995). Also, to the extent that men are generally more satisfied with the marital situation, they may be less likely to complain to their partners and they have less to lose by withdrawing from conflict when the wives want to discuss their issues (Fitzpatrick and Mulac, 1995).

In addition to conflict handling being related to overall relationship satisfaction, another reason for considering how couples handle conflict is that recent research indicates that those couples who do not adequately deal with conflicts are at greater risk for relationship violence. Gryl (1991) examined the relationship between first-year college students' reports of dating violence and how they handled relationship conflicts. Participants in violent relationships were more likely than those in nonviolent relationships to report having relationship conflicts. Moreover, those in violent relationships used more indirect emotional appeals as negotiation strategies, and relied on confrontation and escape-avoidance as coping strategies. Babcock, Waltz, Jacobson, and Gottman

(1993) similarly found a greater likelihood of the demand-withdraw pattern and husband's violence toward their wives. However, the violent marriages were specific to those relationships in which it was the husband's issue (demand) that was ignored by the wife (withdrawal) rather than the reverse.

All of the previous examples of studies examining the link between processes of conflict and relationship satisfaction have been carried out with adult dating or married couples. To our knowledge, there are no corresponding studies looking at the communication correlates of relationship quality among dating adolescents. We hypothesize that the same sorts of factors related to satisfaction in adult romantic relationships will be found in adolescents' dating relationships. Moreover, we expect that those adolescents whose romantic relationships share many of these features will be best prepared to enjoy happy love relationships later in life.

Fostering Intimacy and Relationship Satisfaction in Adolescent Romantic Relationships

Interventions Aimed at Improving Romantic Relationships. A few experimental intervention programs have been designed to improve some of the factors related to relationship satisfaction. For example, experimental mixed-gender programs aimed at preventing dating violence have been successful in modifying the attitudes of both high school students (Jaffe, 1992; Lavoie, Vezina, Piche, and Boivin, 1995) and college students (Holcomb, Sarvela, Sondag, and Holcomb, 1993). In addition to endeavoring to change attitudes, intervention programs have also been aimed at improving social skills. Workshops can help adolescents develop their perspective-taking, negotiation, and listening skills (Christopher, Nangle, and Hansen, 1993; Hansen, Christopher, and Nangle, 1992; Heitland, 1986). For example, Heitland (1986) implemented an experimental training program in premarital communication with high school seniors and college undergraduates. After participating in the program, both young women and young men showed increased competence on measures of communication effectiveness, including listening, self-expression, and joint problem solving. Heitland's intervention program as well as those previously cited were pilot programs. Additional research is needed to identify more specifically the components of a successful program as well as their long-term impact on love relationships. The preliminary findings from the intervention studies suggest that we can teach young women and men how to communicate and relate better with one another.

In addition to implementing intervention programs during junior high school years, another potentially helpful strategy for fostering heterosocial skills is the encouragement of cross-gender cooperation and friendships earlier in life. This idea is explored next.

Linking Cross-Gender Friendships and Romantic Relationships. To the extent that girls and boys learn to form reciprocal, egalitarian friendships with one another in adolescence, they may be better prepared to develop reciprocal, egalitarian love relationships in adulthood. In other words, we contend that love relationships are apt to be most satisfying when a person's romantic partner is also her or his best friend (see Hendrick and Hendrick, 1993). Our premise is consistent with the more general idea that adolescents' romantic relationships are influenced by their prior relationships (Connolly and Johnson, 1996; Furman and Wehner, 1994). Most adolescents' role models for close relationships likely come from their parents and same-gender friends (Connolly and Johnson, 1996). To the extent that parents provide traditionally imbalanced role models (Leaper, Anderson, and Sanders, 1997) and that same-gender friends provide gender-stereotyped patterns (Leaper, 1994), young women and men are apt to learn different ways of interpreting and acting in social relationships. In contrast, having close cross-gender friendships during childhood and adolescence may provide the basis for easier cross-gender romantic relationships during adolescence and adulthood. We can only pose this idea as a hypothesis, however, given the absence of relevant research on cross-gender friendship and its correlates during adolescence.

What we do know about cross-gender friendship is based primarily on work carried out with post-adolescent college students. Contrary to some earlier speculation that male dominance may be an obstacle in cross-gender friendships (McWilliams and Howard, 1993; O'Meara, 1989), subsequent research indicates that cross-gender friendships are typically egalitarian relationships (Monsour, Beard, Harris, and Kurzweil, 1994). Thus, to the extent that young women and men participate in nonsexual friendships together during adolescence, they may learn to integrate the social orientations that traditionally get bifurcated during childhood. Young men may learn to express their feelings more openly as well as develop supportive communication skills. Reciprocally, young women may learn to assert their wishes more directly and develop their instrumental interests. Through these experiences, both women and men may be better prepared to enter intimate, egalitarian romantic relationships with one another.

To date, no longitudinal or retrospective studies have tested our hypothesis that those adolescents who have close cross-gender friends are more likely to experience satisfying romantic relationships later in life. There is evidence, however, that suggests that sharing similar social norms and social orientations emphasizing closeness and equality in childhood and adolescence may benefit the quality of one's romantic relationships later in adulthood. This evidence comes from some recent work indicating that lesbian relationships are more likely than heterosexual or gay men's love relationships to share many of the features of friendship—most notably, equality and reciprocity (Bell and Weinberg, 1978; Blumstein and Schwartz, 1983; Clunis and Green, 1988; Peplau and Cochran, 1990; Peplau, Veniegas, and Campbell, 1995). We speculate that part of this difference may result from lesbians having shared similar gender-related social norms and social orientations emphasizing equality and intimacy during childhood and early adolescence. Indeed, women in general appear more concerned than men with pursuing egalitarian relationships. For example, when asked to consider what they would do if they benefited in an inequitable manner in their relationship, women were more likely than men to indicate that they would make efforts to restore equity in the relationship; men were more likely than women to indicate that they would do nothing (Sprecher, 1992). The results are generally consistent with developmental studies of children and adolescents that found that girls are more likely than boys to emphasize symmetry and mutual collaboration in their same-gender friendships (see Leaper, 1994; Youniss and Smollar, 1985). Thus, we further speculate that similar outcomes would occur for *all* types of romantic relationships if boys as well as girls grew up learning to value closeness and mutuality in relationships. Also, we expect that asymmetries in power and status between women and men would be reduced if girls and boys grew up learning to share control over roles and activities in a cooperative manner. We hope these ideas will receive more attention in future research.

Conclusions: Bringing Women and Men Together

If the premises and arguments in this chapter are accepted, then the reader may wonder how to implement them. Therefore, we close our chapter with two interrelated recommendations. First, family members and educators can make a more concerted effort to make cross-gender cooperation a regular part of children's and adolescents' daily experience. Although favoring same-gender peers may be an inevitable part of children's development, it is possible to increase cooperative cross-gender interactions that may lead to friendships. Studies show that children will interact cooperatively with the other gender when adults provide a structured context that encourages it (for example, Serbin, Tonick, and Sternglanz, 1977). Thus, situations can be arranged that allow children and adolescents to learn from the other gender (see Leaper, 1994). Second, schools and community organizations can institute training workshops to help prepare adolescents for intimate relationships. In light of contemporary concerns with teenage pregnancy and dating and marital violence, as well as with AIDS and other sexually transmitted diseases, we must seek ways to teach young women and men how to communicate and relate better with one another. As our review has highlighted, we are only beginning to investigate the kinds of factors related to adolescent romantic relationships.

Note

1. Consistent with the policy of at least two research journals (*Sex Roles* and *Journal of Social and Personal Relationships*), we use the word *gender* to refer broadly to one's assignment as a female or a male. In contrast, the word *sex* is viewed as referring more explicitly to hypothesized or known biological factors. This chapter does not address potential biological influences on adolescents' romantic relationships. Therefore, we use the term *gender* exclusively throughout. Additionally, rather than use the phrase *opposite gender* (which perpetuates the stereotype that women and men are "opposites"), we deliberately use the terms *cross gender* or *other gender*.

References

Anderson, K. J., and Leaper, C. "Emotion Talk Between Same- and Cross-Gender Friends: Form Follows Function." Unpublished manuscript, 1997.

Babcock, J. C., Waltz, J., Jacobson, N. S., and Gottman, J. M. "Power and Violence: The Relation Between Communication Patterns, Power Discrepancies, and Domestic Violence." *Journal of Consulting and Clinical Psychology*, 1993, *61*, 40–50.

Bachman, R., and Pillemer, K. A. "Epidemiology and Family Violence Involving Adults." In R. T. Ammerman and M. Hersen (eds.), *Assessment of Family Violence: A Clinical and Legal Sourcebook*. New York: Wiley, 1992.

Bagarozzi, D., and Giddings, C. "Conjugal Violence: A Critical Review of Current Research and Clinical Practices." *American Journal of Family Therapy*, 1983, *11*, 3–15.

Bell, A. P., and Weinberg, M. S. *Homosexualities: A Study of Diversity Among Men and Women*. New York: Simon & Schuster, 1978.

Bergman, L. "Dating Violence Among High School Students." *Social Work*, 1992, *37*, 21–27.

Bergman, S. G. "Men's Psychological Development: A Relational Perspective." In R. F. Levant and W. S. Pollack (eds.), *A New Psychology of Men*. New York: Basic Books, 1995.

Berndt, T. J. "Friendship and Friends' Influence in Adolescence." *Current Directions in Psychological Science*, 1992, *1*, 156–159.

Bischoping, K. "Gender Differences in Conversation Topics, 1922–1990." *Sex Roles*, 1993, *28*, 1–18.

Bjorkqvist, K., Osterman, K., and Kaukiainen, A. "The Development of Direct and Indirect Aggressive Strategies in Males and Females." In K. Bjorkqvist and P. Niemela (eds.), *Of Mice and Women: Aspects of Female Aggression*. Orlando: Academic Press, 1992.

Blumstein, P., and Schwartz, P. *American Couples: Money, Work, Sex*. New York: Morrow, 1983.

Bograd, M. "A Feminist Examination of Family Systems Models of Violence Against Women in the Family." In M. Ault-Riche (ed.), *Women and Family Therapy*. Gaithersburg, Md.: Aspen, 1986.

Buhrmester, D., and Furman, W. "The Development of Companionship and Intimacy." *Child Development*, 1987, *58*, 1101–1113.

Burleson, B. R., and Samter, W. "The Social Skills Approach to Relationship Maintenance: How Individual Differences in Communication Skills Affect the Achievement of Relationship Functions." In D. J. Canary and L. Stafford (eds.), *Communication and Relational Maintenance*. Orlando: Academic Press, 1994.

Camarena, P. M., Sarigiani, P. A., and Petersen, A. C. "Gender-Specific Pathways to Intimacy in Early Adolescence." *Journal of Youth and Adolescence*, 1990, *19*, 19–32.

Carlson, B. E. "Dating Violence: A Research Review and Comparison with Spouse Abuse." *Social Casework*, 1987, *68*, 16–23.

Carlson, B. E. "Domestic Violence." In A. Gitterman (ed.), *Handbook of Social Work Practice with Vulnerable Populations*. New York: Columbia University Press, 1991.

Carter, J., Stacey, W. A., and Shupe, A. W. "Male Violence Against Women: Assessment of the Generational Transfer Hypothesis." *Deviant Behavior*, 1988, *9*, 259–273.

Christopher, J. S., Nangle, D. W., and Hansen, D. J. "Social-Skills Interventions with Adolescents: Current Issues and Procedures." *Behavior Modification*, 1993, *17*, 314–338.

Clunis, D. M., and Green, G. D. *Lesbian Couples*. Seattle: Seal Press, 1988.

Connolly, J. A., and Johnson, A. M. "Adolescents' Romantic Relationships and the Structure and Quality of Their Close Interpersonal Ties." *Personal Relationships*, 1996, *3*, 185–195.

Crick, N. R., and Grotpeter, J. K. "Relational Aggression, Gender, and Social-Psychological Adjustment." *Child Development*, 1995, *66*, 710–722.

Deaux, K., and Major, B. "Putting Gender into Context: An Interactive Model of Gender-Related Behavior." *Psychological Review*, 1987, *94*, 369–389.

Department of Health and Human Services. *Sexually Transmitted Disease Surveillance, 1995.* Atlanta: U.S. Dept. of Health and Human Services, Public Health Service, Centers for Disease Control, Center for Prevention Services, Division of STD/HIV Prevention, Surveillance and Information Systems Branch, 1996.

Dindia, K., and Allen, M. "Sex Differences in Self-Disclosure: A Meta-Analysis." *Psychological Bulletin,* 1992, *112,* 106–124.

Fagot, B. I. "Parenting Boys and Girls." In M. H. Bornstein (ed.), *Handbook of Parenting,* Vol. 1: *Children and Parenting.* Hillsdale, N.J.: Erlbaum, 1995.

Federal Bureau of Investigation. *Uniform Crime Reports.* Washington, D.C.: U.S. Department of Justice, 1991.

Feiring, C. "Concepts of Romance in Fifteen-Year-Old Adolescents." *Journal of Research on Adolescence,* 1995, *6,* 181–200.

Felmlee, D. H. "Who's on Top? Power in Romantic Relationships." *Sex Roles,* 1994, *31,* 275–295.

Fitzpatrick, M. A., and Mulac, A. "Relating to Spouse and Stranger: Gender-Preferential Language Use." In P. J. Kalbfleisch and M. J. Cody (eds.), *Gender, Power, and Communication in Human Relationships.* Hillsdale, N.J.: Erlbaum, 1995.

Follingstad, D. R., Rutledge, L. L., McNeill-Harkins, K., and Polek, D. S. "Factors Related to Physical Violence in Dating Relationships." In E. C. Viano (ed.), *Intimate Violence: Interdisciplinary Perspectives.* Bristol, Pa.: Hemisphere, 1992.

Furman, W. "Theory Is Not a Four-Letter Word: Needed Directions in the Study of Adolescent Friendships." In B. Laursen (ed.), *Close Friendships in Adolescence.* New Directions for Child Development, no. 60. San Francisco: Jossey-Bass, 1993.

Furman, W., and Wehner, E. A. "Romantic Views: Toward a Theory of Adolescent Romantic Relationships." In R. Montemayor, G. R. Adams, and T. P. Gullotta (eds.), *Personal Relationships During Adolescence.* Advances in Adolescent Development, vol. 6. Thousand Oaks, Calif.: Sage, 1994.

Gottman, J. M. "The Roles of Conflict Engagement, Escalation, and Avoidance in Marital Interaction: A Longitudinal View of Five Types of Couples." *Journal of Consulting and Clinical Psychology,* 1993, *61,* 6–15.

Gottman, J. M. *"What Predicts Divorce? The Relationship Between Marital Processes and Marital Outcomes.* Hillsdale, N.J.: Erlbaum, 1994.

Gottman, J. M., and Carrere, S. "Why Can't Men and Women Get Along? Developmental Roots and Marital Inequities." In D. J. Canary and L. Stafford (eds.), *Communication and Relational Maintenance.* Orlando: Academic Press, 1994.

Gottman, J. M., and Levenson, R. W. "The Social Psychophysiology of Marriage." In P. Noller and M. A. Fitzpatrick (eds.), *Perspectives on Marital Interaction.* Clevedon, England: Multilingual Matters, 1988.

Gove, W. R., Style, C. B., and Hughes, M. "The Effect of Marriage on the Well-Being of Adults: A Theoretical Analysis." *Journal of Family Issues,* 1990, *11,* 4–35.

Gryl, F. E. "Close Dating Relationships Among College Students: Differences by Use of Violence and by Gender." *Journal of Social and Personal Relationships,* 1991, *8,* 243–264.

Hansen, D. J., Christopher, J. S., and Nangle, D. W. "Adolescent Heterosocial Interactions and Dating." In V. B. Van Hasselt and M. Hersen (eds.), *Handbook of Social Development: A Lifespan Perspective.* New York: Plenum, 1992.

Heavey, C. L., Christensen, A., and Malamuth, N. M. "The Longitudinal Impact of Demand and Withdrawal During Marital Conflict." *Journal of Consulting and Clinical Psychology,* 1995, *63,* 797–801.

Hecht, M. L., Marston, P. J., and Larkey, L. K. "Love Ways and Relationship Quality in Heterosexual Relationships." *Journal of Social and Personal Relationships,* 1994, *11,* 25–43.

Heitland, W. "An Experimental Communication Program for Premarital Dating Couples." *School Counselor,* 1986, *34,* 57–61.

Hendrick, S. S. "Self-Disclosure and Marital Satisfaction." *Journal of Personality and Social Psychology,* 1981, *40,* 1150–1159.

Hendrick, S. S., and Hendrick, C. "Lovers as Friends." *Journal of Social and Personal Relationships*, 1993, *10*, 459–466.

Henley, N. M. "Body Politics Revisited: What Do We Know Today?" In P. J. Kalbfleisch and M. J. Cody (eds.), *Gender, Power, and Communication in Human Relationships*. Hillsdale, N.J.: Erlbaum, 1995.

Hill, C. T., and Stull, D. E. "Gender and Self-Disclosure: Strategies for Exploring the Issues." In V. J. Derlega and J. H. Berg (eds.), *Self-Disclosure: Theory, Research, and Therapy*. New York: Plenum, 1987.

Holcomb, D. R., Sarvela, P. D., Sondag, K. A., and Holcomb, L. H. "An Evaluation of a Mixed-Gender Date Rape Prevention Workshop." *Journal of American College Health*, 1993, *41*, 159–164.

Jaffe, P. G. "An Evaluation of a Secondary School Primary Prevention Program on Violence in Intimate Relationships." *Violence and Victims*, 1992, *7*, 129–146.

Jezl, D. R. "Physical, Sexual and Psychological Abuse in High School Dating Relationships: Prevalence Rates and Self-Esteem Issues." *Child and Adolescent Social Work Journal*, 1996, *13*, 69–87.

Knox, D., and Wilson, K. "Dating Problems of University Students." *College Student Journal*, 1983, *17*, 225–228.

Koss, M. P., and Dinero, T. E. "Predictors of Sexual Aggression Among a National Sample of Male College Students." In R. A. Prentky and V. L. Quinsey (eds.), *Human Sexual Aggression: Current Perspectives* (special issue). *Annals of the New York Academy of Sciences*, 1988, *528*, 133–146.

Kurdek, L. A., and Schmitt, J. P. "Relationship Quality of Partners in Heterosexual Married, Heterosexual Cohabiting, and Gay and Lesbian Relationships." *Journal of Personality and Social Psychology*, 1986, *51*, 711–720.

Laner, M. R. "Violence and Its Precipitators: Which Is More Likely to Be Identified as a Dating Problem?" *Deviant Behavior*, 1990, *11*, 319–329.

Lavoie, F., Vezina, L., Piche, C., and Boivin, M. "Evaluation of a Prevention Program for Violence in Teen Dating Relationships." *Journal of Interpersonal Violence*, 1995, *10*, 516–524.

Leaper, C. "Exploring the Consequences of Gender Segregation on Social Relationships." In C. Leaper (ed.), *Childhood Gender Segregation: Causes and Consequences*. New Directions for Child Development, no. 65. San Francisco: Jossey-Bass, 1994.

Leaper, C. "Constructing Representations of Gender in the Classroom [Review of *Gender Identities and Education: The Impact of Starting School*]." *American Journal of Psychology*, 1995, *108*, 300–304.

Leaper, C., Anderson, K. J., and Sanders, P. "Moderators of Gender Effects on Parents' Talk to Their Children: A Meta-Analysis." *Developmental Psychology*, 1997, *33*.

Leaper, C., Carson, M., Baker, C., Holliday, H., and Myers, S. B. "Self-Disclosure and Listener Verbal Support in Same-Gender and Cross-Gender Friends' Conversations." *Sex Roles*, 1995, *33*, 387–404.

Leaper, C., and Holliday, H. "Gossip in Same-Gender and Cross-Gender Friends' Conversations." *Personal Relationships*, 1995, *2*, 237–246.

Levant, R. F. "Toward the Reconstruction of Masculinity." In R. F. Levant and W. S. Pollack (eds.), *A New Psychology of Men*. New York: Basic Books, 1995.

Levy, B. "Abusive Teen Dating Relationships: An Emerging Issue for the Nineties." *Response to the Victimization of Women and Children*, 1990, *13*, 5.

Lockheed, M. E. "Some Determinants and Consequences of Sex Segregation in the Classroom." In L. C. Wilkinson and C. B. Marrett (eds.), *Gender Influences in Classroom Interaction*. Orlando: Academic Press, 1985.

Lundberg-Love, P., and Geffner, R. "Date Rape: Prevalence, Risk Factors, and a Proposed Model." In M. A. Pirog-Good and J. E. Stets (eds.), *Violence in Dating Relationships: Emerging Social Issues*. New York: Praeger, 1989.

Maccoby, E. E. "Gender and Relationships: A Developmental Account." *American Psychologist*, 1990, *45*, 513–520.

Maccoby, E. E. "Commentary: Gender Segregation in Childhood." In C. Leaper (ed.), *Childhood Gender Segregation: Causes and Consequences*. New Directions for Child Development, no. 65. San Francisco: Jossey-Bass, 1994.

McKenry, P. C., and Price, S. J. "Divorce: Are Men at Risk?" In D. Moore and Fred Leafgren (eds.), *Problem-Solving Strategies and Interventions for Men in Conflict*. Alexandria, Va.: American Association for Counseling and Development, 1990.

McWilliams, S., and Howard, J. A. "Solidarity and Hierarchy in Cross-Sex Friendships." *Journal of Social Issues*, 1993, *49*, 191–202.

Messner, M. A., and Sabo, D. F. *Sex, Violence and Power in Sports: Rethinking Masculinity*. Freedom, Calif.: Crossing Press. 1994.

Miedzian, M. *Boys Will Be Boys: Breaking the Link Between Masculinity and Violence*. New York: Doubleday, 1991.

Miller, P. M., Danaher, D. L., and Forbes, D. "Sex-Related Strategies for Coping with Interpersonal Conflict in Children Aged Five to Seven." *Developmental Psychology*, 1986, *22*, 543–548.

Monsour, M., Beard, C., Harris, B., and Kurzweil, N. "Challenges Confronting Cross-Sex Friendships: Much Ado About Nothing?" *Sex Roles*, 1994, *31*, 55–77.

Murray, C. "Conservatism and Improvement in Social Conditions: Responses to Questions About U.S. Stability and the Future of America." *Commentary*, 1995, *100*, 87–88.

National Center for Health Statistics. *Incidence of Divorce: 1975–1988*. Washington, D.C.: U.S. Government Printing Office, 1989.

National Center for Health Statistics. *Monthly Vital Statistics Report*. Washington, D.C.: U.S. Government Printing Office, Sept. 1993.

Nelson, M. B. *The Stronger Women Get, the More Men Like Football: Sexism and the American Culture of Sports*. Orlando: Harcourt, Brace, 1994.

Noller, P. "Gender and Emotional Communication in Marriage: Different Cultures or Differential Social Power?" *Journal of Language and Social Psychology*, 1993, *12*, 132–152.

O'Keeffe, N. K., Brockopp, K., and Chew, E. "Teen Dating Violence." *Social Work*, 1986, *31*, 465–468.

O'Meara, J. D. "Cross-Sex Friendship: Four Basic Challenges of an Ignored Relationship." *Sex Roles*, 1989, *21*, 525–543.

Parsons, T., and Bales, R. E. *Family Socialization and Interaction Process*. New York: Free Press, 1955.

Peplau, L. A., and Cochran, S. D. "A Relationship Perspective on Homosexuality." In D. P. McWhirter, S. A. Sanders, and J. M. Reinisch (eds.), *Homosexuality/Heterosexuality: Concepts of Sexual Orientation*. New York: Oxford University Press, 1990.

Peplau, L. A., Veniegas, R. C., and Campbell, S. M. "Gay and Lesbian Relationships." In R. C. Savin-Williams and K. M. Cohen (eds.), *The Lives of Lesbians, Gays, and Bisexuals*. Orlando: Harcourt Brace, 1995.

Reisman, J. M. "Intimacy in Same-Sex Friendships." *Sex Roles*, 1990, *23*, 65–82.

Reuterman, N. A., and Burcky, W. D. "Dating Violence in High School: A Profile of the Victims." *Psychology: A Journal of Human Behavior*, 1989, *26*, 1–9.

Sadker, M., and Sadker, D. *Failing at Fairness: How America's Schools Cheat Girls*. New York: Scribner, 1994.

Serbin, L. A., Tonick, I. J., and Sternglanz, S. "Shaping Cooperative Cross-Sex Play." *Child Development*, 1977, *48*, 924–929.

Sharabany, R., Gershoni, R., and Hofman, J. E. "Girlfriend, Boyfriend: Age and Sex Differences in Intimate Friendships." *Developmental Psychology*, 1981, *17*, 800–808.

Sollie, D. L., and Fischer, J. L. "Sex-Role Orientation, Intimacy of Topic, and Target Person Differences in Self-Disclosure Among Women." *Sex Roles*, 1985, *12*, 917–929.

Sprecher, S. "How Men and Women Expect to Feel and Behave in Response to Inequity in Close Relationships." *Social Psychology Quarterly*, 1992, *55*, 57–69.

Straus, M. A., and Gelles, R. J. "Violence in American Families: How Much Is There and Why Does It Occur?" In E. W. Nunnally, C. S. Chilman, and F. M. Cox (eds.), *Troubled Relationships*. Families In Trouble Series, vol. 3. Thousand Oaks, Calif.: Sage, 1988.

Tannen, D. *You Just Don't Understand: Women and Men in Conversation.* New York: Morrow, 1990.

White, J. W., and Humphrey, J. A. "Women's Aggression in Heterosexual Conflicts." *Aggressive Behavior,* 1994, *20,* 195–202.

White, J. W., and Koss, M. P. "Adolescent Sexual Aggression Within Heterosexual Relationships: Prevalence, Characteristics, and Causes." In H. E. Barbaree, W. L. Marshall, and S. M. Hudson (eds.), *The Juvenile Sex Offender.* New York: Guilford Press, 1993.

Winn, K. I., Crawford, D. W., and Fischer, J. L. "Equity and Commitment in Romance Versus Friendship." *Journal of Social Behavior and Personality,* 1991, *6,* 301–314.

Wood, W., Rhodes, N., and Whelan, M. "Sex Differences in Positive Well-Being: A Consideration of Emotional Style and Marital Status." *Psychological Bulletin,* 1989, *106,* 249–264.

Youniss, J., and Smollar, J. *Adolescents' Relations with Their Mothers, Fathers, and Peers.* Chicago: University of Chicago Press, 1985.

CAMPBELL LEAPER is associate professor of psychology, University of California, Santa Cruz.

KRISTIN J. ANDERSON is a doctoral candidate in psychology at the University of California, Santa Cruz.

Limited research exists on romantic relationships in adolescence. The chapters in this volume call attention to several conceptual issues that must be addressed to advance understanding of processes and development in adolescent romantic relationships.

Afterword: Romantic Relationships in Adolescence—More Than Casual Dating

Shmuel Shulman, W. Andrew Collins, Danielle Knafo

Romantic relationships in early and middle adolescence frequently appear in fiction and autobiographies. In some cases they are described as superficial or awkward and are understood in terms of an experience rather than as a relationship (Furman and Wehner, this volume). Dunphy's (1963) pioneering work described how early interactions with the opposite sex often occur within the context of a crowd, thereby enabling girls and boys to develop a sense of comfort following the previous years of gender segregation (Leaper and Anderson, this volume). Yet such encounters, which in many cases are of short duration, are perceived as casual dating and are considered less enduring relationships or are examined as such (Hinde and Stevenson-Hinde, 1987). In addition, the weaker sense of commitment among adolescent romantic partners also leads to considering these relationships as superficial. The majority of extant work has primarily consisted of demographic studies of dating patterns and has dealt less with development of adolescent romantic relationships. Particularly lacking has been a theoretical framework to guide research on romantic relationships during this developmental stage (Furman and Wehner, 1994).

The premise of this volume is that romantic relationships in adolescence (even when they do not last for more than two months) represent patterns of dyadic interaction that are governed by enduring principles. This final chapter underscores three themes from the chapters in this volume that speak to systemic and developmental perspectives on the common features and processes in the study of close relationships. The first theme addresses the possible common features that regulate relationships. The second theme concerns the interplay between romantic relationships and other significant relationships (such as with parents and peers) in adolescence and the ways these relationships change over time. The third theme deals with the carryover of current and former close relationships to romantic relationships in adolescence.

Basic Features of Romantic Relationships

In their proposed theory on adolescent romantic relationships, Furman and Wehner (1994) suggest that "romantic partners become major figures in the functioning of the attachment, caregiving, affiliative, and sexual reproduction behavioral systems" (p. 177). Features that coordinate close relationships in various contexts and stages of life play a role in relationships of adolescents with their romantic partners.

In their seminal work, Ainsworth, Blehar, Waters, and Wall (1978) describe two dimensions that characterize an attachment relationship. The first is the proximity and contact between mother and infant. The second is the infant's level of exploration while knowing that the mother is available. Conceptually, this balance reflects the optimal coordination between partners in a relationship. Proximity is maintained but not at the expense of individuality. Rather, it supports and facilitates partners' individuality.

Interaction between adolescent romantic partners, as described by Shulman, Levy-Shiff, Kedem, and Alon in Chapter Three, demonstrates how the balance between proximity and exploration organizes this relational context. Interdependent romantic partners displayed a relationship that emphasized more emotional closeness and less control. Disengaged romantic partners, conversely, reported a lower level of emotional closeness and a higher level of control. In the interdependent type, partners are attracted to each other by their sense of closeness and respect. In the disengaged type, where closeness is less expressed or experienced, partners must employ control to keep the relationship from falling apart.

Seiffge-Krenke, in Chapter Four, shows that healthy adolescents seek intimacy, companionship, nurturance, and affection with their romantic partner while remaining at ease in dealing with conflicts. Diabetic adolescents, were also found to perceive their romantic partners as a source of security in that they provide companionship and intimacy. Yet they emphasized their wishes for harmonious understanding by their partners and tended to avoid conflicts.

In Chapter Six, Leaper and Anderson present a conceptual review of what accounts for a satisfying romantic relationship. Egalitarian relationships characterized by equal distribution of power and mutual self-disclosure allow each partner the opportunity to receive some validation from the other. Research indicates an additional important predictor of relationship satisfaction and adjustment in the pair's capacity to engage in conversations about their disagreements (Gottman, 1993). Moreover, relationship satisfaction is strongly tied to the ability of one partner to bring up disagreements without the other partner either withdrawing or countercomplaining. In reality, many pairs described imbalances in decision making and emotional involvement (Felm-lee, 1994).

Thus the balance (or imbalance) between being close to the romantic part-ner and insisting on a distinct entity is manifested in different forms among romantic partners. A mature intimate romantic relationship should encompass "closeness with distinctive boundaries" (Williamson, 1982, p. 310). Concep-tually, Karpel's (1976) analysis of different types of relationships is consistent with our suggestion. In a mature form of an intimate relationship, "dialogue" and "individuality" are well developed and integrated. Partners respond to each other as wholes, respect each other's needs and thoughts, cope with disagree-ments, and affirm, deepen, and maintain the relationship through dialogue. In immature relationships, partners lack a sense of individuality and self-agency and the attitude toward the other is reflected in increased dependence on the other or a penchant for disengagement.

The Interplay Between Romantic Relationships, Family Relationships, and Relationships with Peers During Adolescent Development

A premise of adolescent development is the growing "apartness" between ado-lescents and their parents evidenced in three domains. First, adolescents spend increasing amounts of time apart from their parents. Second, adolescents feel that parents are not as close to them as they were in the past. Third, adoles-cents invest more time with, and are increasingly closer to, their age-mates. Distancing from parents, however, takes place within the context of closeness. Parents remain a major source of support for their adolescent children even though the salience of peers increases (Youniss and Smollar, 1985).

Emerging from a social exchange theory, Laursen and Williams, Chapter One, show that frequency of interaction and diversity of activity with parents, siblings, and same-sex friends decreases during adolescence, whereas those with opposite-sex friends increase. Similarly, Furman and Wehner, Chapter Two, report that romantic partners rank below parents and same-sex peers as sources of support during early stages of adolescence. In middle adolescence, romantic partners tied for second with mothers. During college, men rated their partners as the most supportive individual in their network, whereas women rated their partners, mothers, friends, and siblings as most supportive. By comparing adolescents with and without romantic partners, Laursen and Williams demonstrate that the changes in the hierarchy of relationships reflect more than the frequency of interactions or expected support. Adolescents with romantic partners are obviously more likely than those without romantic part-ners to indicate that these relationships are close, interdependent, and influ-ential, and that they contain a substantial amount of social interaction and shared activities. As adolescents grow older, romantic relationships are increas-ingly apt to take the lead over other relationships in characteristics that reflect interdependence. Thus romantic relationships appear to alter the dynamics of other relationships, representing a more egalitarian type of closeness.

These findings raise the possibility that the consolidation of a romantic interdependent relationship may affirm an adolescent's sense of identity (Erikson, 1963) and hence his or her feeling of "being a separate entity." This individual change may stimulate positive transformations in relationships with parents (Collins, 1995). Results presented by Furman and Wehner in Chapter Two support the hypothesis of a link between changes in these different types of relationships. In a high school sample, perceptions of relationships with romantic partners were uncorrelated with perceptions of relationships with parents, whereas the two types of relationships were correlated in a sample of college students.

Though same-sex friends are central figures in the life of adolescents, their salience decreases as adolescents become more committed to their romantic relationships. This is evident in the decreased investment in same-sex friendships (Laursen and Williams, Chapter One). Moreover, Shulman and his colleagues, in Chapter Three, also report an inverse relation between relationships with romantic partners and those with close friends: the greater a male's feeling of closeness to his same-sex friend, tolerance of the friend's differing views, and respect for him, the less close he is to his girlfriend and the less he respects her individuality. Examining this web of adolescent close relationships from a developmental perspective reveals the changing interrelations among the multiple relationships in which adolescents participate.

Carryover from Former Relationships to Future Relationships

Carryover of relationships is central to Bowlby's (1973) theory: models of self and others and relationships that develop from experience in primary and early relationships influence the nature of interaction with the environment and expectations concerning availability, responsiveness, and attitudes of others, as well as expectations about the self in relationships (Sroufe and Fleeson, 1986).

In the findings reported by Collins, Hennighausen, Schmit, and Sroufe in Chapter Five, the frequency and quality of interactions with friends during middle childhood predicted security with dating partners at age sixteen. Links between earlier experiences and later functioning is not always direct. Dating security and intimacy at age sixteen were also mediated by the capacity to disclose inner feelings at age fifteen, and these in turn related to social competence in middle childhood. These results point to the dynamics of carryover. "Carrying forward all of the specific behaviors and response chains from previous interactions would be an overwhelming task, but a limited set of expectations can generate countless behavioral reactions, flexibly employed in a variety of situations" (Sroufe and Fleeson, 1986, p. 86). Results further hint that more specific skills are also carried forward. Following gender boundary rules during preadolescence was related to later onset of sexual activity. Together these findings imply that the particular behaviors that constitute an adolescent's romantic relationship and the quality of experiences associated with those behaviors are embedded in the history of previous relationships.

Conclusions

The chapters in this volume reflect a strong emerging conviction that romantic relationships in adolescence can be understood more fully in the context of close relationships with significant others in the present and in the past. The descriptions of empirical and conceptual advances have underscored some key issues that provide a basis for future research. Studying adolescent romantic relationships requires attention to different behavioral and affective features as well as to the balance between partners' joint and individual needs. In addition, understanding the links between romantic relationships and other significant relationships during various stages of adolescence may shed light on how romantic relationships develop from casual encounters toward attachments. Finally, establishing the links between early and intermediate close relationships and the emergence of romantic relationships in adolescence informs us about a central relationship in adolescent development that heretofore has been underresearched.

References

Ainsworth, M.D.S., Blehar, M., Waters, E., and Wall, S. *Patterns of Attachment.* Hillsdale, N.J.: Erlbaum, 1978.

Bowlby, J. *Attachment and Loss,* Vol. 2: *Separation.* New York: Basic Books, 1973.

Collins, W. A. "Relationships and Development: Family Adaptation to Individual Change." In S. Shulman (ed.), *Close Relationships and Socioemotional Development.* Norwood, N.J.: Ablex, 1995.

Dunphy, D.C. "The Social Structure of Urban Adolescent Peer Groups." *Sociometry,* 1963, *26,* 230–246.

Erikson, E. H. *Childhood and Society.* New York: Norton, 1963.

Felmlee, D. H. "Who Is on Top? Power in Romantic Relationships." *Sex Roles,* 1994, *31,* 275–295.

Furman, W., and Wehner, E. A. "Romantic Views: Toward a Theory of Adolescent Romantic Relationships." In R. Montemayor, G. R. Adams, and T. P. Gullotta (eds.), *Personal Relationships During Adolescence.* Thousand Oaks, Calif.: Sage, 1994.

Gottman, J. M. "The Role of Conflict Engagement, Escalation, and Avoidance in Marital Interaction: A Longitudinal View of Five Types of Couples." *Journal of Consulting and Clinical Psychology,* 1993, *61,* 6–15.

Hinde, R. A., and Stevenson-Hinde, J. "Interpersonal Relationships and Child Development." *Developmental Review,* 1978, *7,* 1–21.

Karpel, M. "Individuation: From Fusion to Dialogue." *Family Process,* 1976, *15,* 65–82.

Sroufe, L. A., and Fleeson, J. "Attachment and the Construction of Relationships." In W. W. Hartup and Z. Rubin (eds.), *Relationships and Development.* Hillsdale, N.J.: Erlbaum, 1986.

Williamson, D. S. "Personal Authority in Family Experience via Termination of the Intergenerational Hierarchial Boundary. Part III: Personal Authority Defined, and the Power of Play in the Change Process." *Journal of Marriage and Family Therapy,* 1982, *8,* 309–323.

Youniss, J., and Smollar, J. *Adolescents' Relations with Their Mothers, Fathers, and Peers.* Chicago: University of Chicago Press, 1985.

SHMUEL SHULMAN is associate professor in the Department of Psychology at Bar Ilan University, Ramat Gan, Israel.

W. ANDREW COLLINS is professor at the Institute of Child Development, University of Minnesota.

DANIELLE KNAFO is senior lecturer in the Department of Psychology at Bar Ilan University, Ramat Gan, Israel.

INDEX

Aboud, F. E., 81, 83
Acker, M., 53, 66
Adolescent Health Survey, 77
Adolescent Interpersonal Competence Questionnaire, 32
Adolescents: capacity for intimacy developed by, 69–84; diabetic, 53–68; and dissatisfied and violent marriages, 87–88; and gender development, 85–103; and health status, 53–68; interdependence and closeness for, 3–20; intimacy for, 37–50; romantic views of, 21–36; sexual activity among, 54; social competence of, 76–77; themes of, 105–110
Affiliation, behavioral systems view of, 22–34
Aggression, and athletics, 89
Ahmed, N., 56, 65
Ahmed, P. I., 56, 65
Aid to Families with Dependent Children, 86
Ainsworth, M.D.S., 71, 82, 106, 109
Allen, J. P., 34, 82
Allen, M., 38, 49, 92, 100
Alon, E., 1, 37, 51, 106
Amidon, E., 38, 47, 49
Anderson, K. J., 1, 47, 85, 89, 94, 97, 99, 101, 103, 105, 106
Anderson Darling, C., 63, 65
Argyle, M., 4, 19
Attachment: behavioral systems view of, 22–34; patterns of, 71–74, 78

Babcock, J. C., 94, 95–96, 99
Bachman, R., 87, 99
Bagarozzi, D., 87, 99
Baker, C., 101
Bales, R. E., 91, 102
Barnett, M., 73, 82
Bartholomew, K., 26, 34
Bartis, S., 50
Beard, C., 97, 102
Behavioral Systems Questionnaire, 27–28, 30
Behavioral systems theory, and romantic views, 22–31
Bell, A. P., 97, 99

Bell, K. L., 82
Bennett, C., 84
Bergeisen, L. G., 77, 82
Bergman, L., 86, 87, 99
Bergman, S. G., 47, 49, 94, 95, 99
Berkeley Adult Attachment Interview, 26, 29, 30
Berndt, F., 38, 47, 49
Berndt, T. J., 90, 99
Berscheid, E., 4, 5, 6, 7, 8, 18, 19, 20
Bierman, K., 72, 82
Bigelow, B. J., 72, 82
Bischoping, K., 93, 95, 99
Bjorkqvist, K., 89, 99
Blehar, M., 71, 82, 106, 109
Blos, P., 37, 49
Blum, R. W., 77, 82
Blumstein, P., 91, 97, 99
Blyth, D. A., 53, 66
Boeger, A., 67
Bograd, M., 87, 99
Boivin, M., 96, 101
Borman-Spurrell, E., 26, 34
Bowlby, J., 25, 34, 70, 82, 108, 109
Brady, J., 81, 83
Brockopp, K., 87, 102
Bronfenbrenner, U., 18, 19
Brown, B. B., 5, 6, 19, 23, 24, 34
Brownlee, J. R., 16, 20
Brunnquell, D., 71, 82
Buhrmester, D., 5, 6, 18, 19, 21n, 24, 29, 34, 34, 35, 55, 57, 64, 66, 90, 99
Burcky, W. D., 88, 102
Burleson, B. R., 91, 99

Camarena, P. M., 38, 40, 49, 90, 99
Campbell, S. M., 97, 102
Cantor, N., 53, 64, 65, 66
Capacity for Vulnerability Scale, 76–77, 78
Card Sort Problem Solving Procedure, 41–42
Caregiving, behavioral systems view of, 22–34
Carlson, B. E., 86, 88, 99
Carlsen, E., 70, 74, 75, 77, 81, 83, 84
Carrere, S., 89, 100
Carson, M., 101

111

ORDERING INFORMATION

NEW DIRECTIONS FOR CHILD DEVELOPMENT is a series of paperback books that presents the latest research findings on all aspects of children's psychological development, including their cognitive, social, moral, and emotional growth. Books in the series are published quarterly in Fall, Winter, Spring, and Summer and are available for purchase by subscription and individually.

PHONE SUBSCRIPTION or single-copy orders toll-free at (888) 378–2537 or at (415) 433–1767 (toll call).

FAX orders toll-free to (800) 605–2665.

SUBSCRIPTIONS cost $65.00 for individuals (a savings of 23 percent over single-copy prices) and $105.00 for institutions, agencies, and libraries. Standing orders are accepted. New York residents, add local sales tax for subscriptions. (For subscriptions outside the United States, add $7.00 for shipping via surface mail or $25.00 for air mail. Orders must be prepaid in U.S. dollars by check drawn on a U.S. bank or charged to VISA, MasterCard, or American Express.)

SINGLE COPIES cost $25.00 plus shipping (see below) when payment accompanies order. California, New Jersey, New York, and Washington, D.C., residents, please include appropriate sales tax. Canadian residents, add GST and any local taxes. Billed orders will be charged shipping and handling. No billed shipments to post office boxes. (Orders from outside the United States must be prepaid in U.S. dollars by check drawn on a U.S. bank or charged to VISA, MasterCard, or American Express.)

SHIPPING (Single Copies Only): $30.00 and under, add $5.50; to $50.00, add $6.50; to $75.00, add $7.50; to $100.00, add $9.00; to $150.00, add $10.00.

ALL PRICES are subject to change.

DISCOUNTS for quantity orders are available. Please write to the address below for information.

ALL ORDERS must include either the name of an individual or an official purchase order number. Please submit your order as follows:
    Subscriptions: specify series and year subscription is to begin
    Single copies: include individual title code (such as CD59)

MAIL ORDERS TO:
Jossey-Bass Publishers
350 Sansome Street
San Francisco, California 94104-1342

FOR SUBSCRIPTION SALES OUTSIDE OF THE UNITED STATES, contact any international subscription agency or Jossey-Bass directly.

UNITED STATES POSTAL SERVICE™

Statement of Ownership, Management, and Circulation
(Required by 39 USC 3685)

1. Publication Title	2. Publication Number									3. Filing Date
NEW DIRECTIONS FOR CHILD DEVELOPMENT	0	1	9	5	_	2	2	6	9	9/26/97

4. Issue Frequency	5. Number of Issues Published Annually	6. Annual Subscription Price
QUARTERLY	4	$ 65 - indiv. $105 - instit.

7. Complete Mailing Address of Known Office of Publication *(Not printer) (Street, city, county, state, and ZIP+4)*

350 SANSOME STREET
SAN FRANCISCO, CA   94104
(SAN FRANCISCO COUNTY)

Contact Person
ROGER HUNT
Telephone
415 782 3232

8. Complete Mailing Address of Headquarters or General Business Office of Publisher *(Not printer)*

(ABOVE ADDRESS)

9. Full Names and Complete Mailing Addresses of Publisher, Editor, and Managing Editor *(Do not leave blank)*

Publisher *(Name and complete mailing address)*

JOSSEY-BASS INC., PUBLISHERS
(ABOVE ADDRESS)

Editor *(Name and complete mailing address)*   WILLIAM DAMON
BROWN UNIVERSITY
EDUCATION DEPARTMENT BOX 1938
PROVIDENCE, RI   02912

Managing Editor *(Name and complete mailing address)*

NONE

10. Owner *(Do not leave blank. If the publication is owned by a corporation, give the name and address of the corporation immediately followed by the names and addresses of all stockholders owning or holding 1 percent or more of the total amount of stock. If not owned by a corporation, give the names and addresses of the individual owners. If owned by a partnership or other unincorporated firm, give its name and address as well as those of each individual owner. If the publication is published by a nonprofit organization, give its name and address.)*

Full Name	Complete Mailing Address
SIMON & SCHUSTER, INC.	P.O. BOX 1172
	ENGLEWOOD CLIFFS, NJ 07632-1172

11. Known Bondholders, Mortgagees, and Other Security Holders Owning or Holding 1 Percent or More of Total Amount of Bonds, Mortgages, or Other Securities. If none, check box ───▶ ☐ None

Full Name	Complete Mailing Address
SAME AS ABOVE	SAME AS ABOVE

12. Tax Status *(For completion by nonprofit organizations authorized to mail at special rates) (Check one)*
The purpose, function, and nonprofit status of this organization and the exempt status for federal income tax purposes:
☐ Has Not Changed During Preceding 12 Months
☐ Has Changed During Preceding 12 Months *(Publisher must submit explanation of change with this statement)*

PS Form **3526**, September 1995 *(See Instructions on Reverse)*

13. Publication Title	14. Issue Date for Circulation Data Below
NEW DIRECTIONS FOR CHILD DEVELOPMENT	SPRING 1997

15. Extent and Nature of Circulation		Average No. Copies Each Issue During Preceding 12 Months	Actual No. Copies of Single Issue Published Nearest to Filing Date
a. Total Number of Copies *(Net press run)*		1333	1366
b. Paid and/or Requested Circulation	(1) Sales Through Dealers and Carriers, Street Vendors, and Counter Sales *(Not mailed)*	160	122
	(2) Paid or Requested Mail Subscriptions *(Include advertiser's proof copies and exchange copies)*	488	519
c. Total Paid and/or Requested Circulation *(Sum of 15b(1) and 15b(2))* ▶		648	641
d. Free Distribution by Mail *(Samples, complimentary, and other free)*		0	0
e. Free Distribution Outside the Mail *(Carriers or other means)*		168	81
f. Total Free Distribution *(Sum of 15d and 15e)* ▶		168	81
g. Total Distribution *(Sum of 15c and 15f)* ▶		816	722
h. Copies not Distributed	(1) Office Use, Leftovers, Spoiled	517	644
	(2) Returns from News Agents	0	0
i. Total *(Sum of 15g, 15h(1), and 15h(2))* ▶		1333	1366
Percent Paid and/or Requested Circulation *(15c / 15g x 100)*		79%	89%

16. Publication of Statement of Ownership
☒ Publication required. Will be printed in the ___WINTER 1997___ issue of this publication.
☐ Publication not required.

17. Signature and Title of Editor, Publisher, Business Manager, or Owner

SUSAN E. LEWIS
PERIODICALS DIRECTOR

Susan E. Lewis [signature]

Date 9/25/97

I certify that all information furnished on this form is true and complete. I understand that anyone who furnishes false or misleading information on this form or who omits material or information requested on the form may be subject to criminal sanctions (including fines and imprisonment) and/or civil sanctions (including multiple damages and civil penalties).

Instructions to Publishers

1. Complete and file one copy of this form with your postmaster annually on or before October 1. Keep a copy of the completed form for your records.

2. In cases where the stockholder or security holder is a trustee, include in items 10 and 11 the name of the person or corporation for whom the trustee is acting. Also include the names and addresses of individuals who are stockholders who own or hold 1 percent or more of the total amount of bonds, mortgages, or other securities of the publishing corporation. In item 11, if none, check the box. Use blank sheets if more space is required.

3. Be sure to furnish all circulation information called for in item 15. Free circulation must be shown in items 15d, e, and f.

4. If the publication had second-class authorization as a general or requester publication, this Statement of Ownership, Management, and Circulation must be published; it must be printed in any issue in October or, if the publication is not published during October, the first issue printed after October.

5. In item 16, indicate the date of the issue in which this Statement of Ownership will be published.

6. Item 17 must be signed.

Failure to file or publish a statement of ownership may lead to suspension of second-class authorization.